# Idea
# Magnets

## 7 Strategies for Cultivating & Attracting Creative Business Leaders

## Mike Brown

ISBN  978-1-7320386-2-2


*Consulting Editor: Tara Baukus Mello*
*Critique Partner: Emma Alvarez Gibson*
*Cover & Interior Design: Be Mello Media, Inc.*
*Illustrations: John D. Chinn*
*Back Cover Photo: Henry Behrens*


For wholesale orders or to order copies in bulk for your conference, company or organization, contact
The Brainzooming Group
info@brainzooming.com
816-509-5320

To all the Idea Magnets in my life
whose stories will be told
beyond this book.


For any of you who are still waiting to
meet the first Idea Magnet in your
life, how about becoming one
yourself, starting today?

# Contents

What is an Idea Magnet?     1

If your Name is Brown, Why is your     6
Color Orange?

The Seven Strategies     10

    Generating Inspiration     15

    Embodying Servant Leadership     30

    Attracting Opposites     47

    Making Unexpected Connections     65

    Encouraging People and Ideas     82

    Implementing for Impact     100

    Recharging Creative Energy     117

Closing the Circuit     131

What's Next?     136

Acknowledgements     139

# 1

# What is an Idea Magnet?

Think about a time when you and your team, your organization, or even your family needed to generate incredibly creative ideas and turn them into reality. Were you able to effectively share an inspiring vision for what you needed to accomplish together? Could everyone find some way to contribute productively? Did the group imaginatively identify resources and innovative ideas to accomplish amazing opportunities?

And if all that happened, was it easy? Or was it a challenge? Was it one of those moments where everything seemed to magically click, but it's never happened again? Or did you collectively fall short in realizing the possibilities you had hoped to accomplish? If you ended up being disappointed, you are far from alone. In fact, it's well within the norm in today's workplaces, schools, and families.

But achieving tremendous creative success as an individual or as a group doesn't have to be rare or depend on some magical combination of things you can't ever recreate.

Idea Magnets, and those around them, experience these types of moments all the time. And there is no magic involved.

### What is an Idea Magnet?

Idea Magnets inspire creative ideas *and* encourage extreme creativity in those around them. Idea Magnets make life more exciting, fulfilling, and successful in everything they touch—from their work, to their personal lives to chance encounters—by applying surprising connections to deliver intriguingly powerful results. They do it all with amazing ease. Idea Magnets serve and lead with boldness and humility. They imagine bold visions and attract other Idea Magnets to help implement them. They make BIG things happen while providing their teams abundant opportunities to grow and recharge their own creative imaginations.

### 11 Signs You're with an Idea Magnet

How do you spot an Idea Magnet? Based on my experiences, Idea Magnets:

1. Absorb diverse, creativity-generating references and resources.
2. Ask rich questions.
3. Listen before they talk.
4. Generalize opportunities and challenges as a way to find comparable situations to expand creative possibilities.
5. Connect people, resources, and ideas in intriguing ways.

6.  Easily move between foreground and background in group settings.
7.  Embrace building on their own and others' ideas to grow their potential.
8.  Are encouraging when a creative idea (as well a fellow Idea Magnet) is new and needs support.
9.  Enthusiastically cheer for others to be successful creatively.
10. Display boldness for stretching what is possible as well as envisioning the impossible.
11. Make challenging decisions when an idea has outlived (or is about to outlive) its usefulness.

As you read these characteristics, I'll bet that certain people you know came to mind. Maybe you even thought of yourself, a company or a group you have some experience with. (Idea Magnets can be individuals, groups, teams, departments, or organizations.)

While you may have also thought of some famous people, there's one thing you should know about the people mentioned here. They aren't big names you see in the press. You won't see stories of the billionaire tech visionaries; the music industry and Hollywood geniuses or the wunderkinds that put in a couple of years at consulting firms and then started their own companies with tons of venture capital.

No, most of the people you will read about here don't make headlines. They are currently Idea Magnets beyond the world's spotlight. While the world might think what they are doing doesn't generate the interest that justifies attention, the world is, quite honestly, missing the point.

The Idea Magnets you'll read about here are creating tremendous impacts—the kinds of impacts we can all aspire to create for those around us.

## The Science of Magnetism

My mission with this book is to help you cultivate your own Idea Magnetism and attract more Idea Magnets to you by increasing your "magnetic field" of creativity. To start, let's spend a moment to refresh how magnetism works to demonstrate how its characteristics and behaviors provide a powerful analogy to attracting smart, creative people.

These days, we think of a magnet as a man-made object we can use to attract certain metals. In reality, a magnet is any object that contains a magnetic field. The earliest magnets recorded were stones that attracted iron—these were called lodestones by the Greeks.

A magnetic field is an invisible force that attracts ferrous metals such as steel, iron, nickel, and even cobalt. This force is an electric field drawing the objects to it and making them "stick." Move that invisible electric field and the object will move along with it.

The result can be as simple as picking up a handful of dropped nails with ease or a stunning artistic dance, such as the dancing iron filings at the Arizona Science Center made by TechnoFrolics.

## Strengthening Your Magnetic Field

In this book, you'll discover seven strategies to help you strengthen your own field of magnetism to cultivate and attract other Idea Magnets. Put these strategies into action to increase your own creativity and the creativity of those around you.

I know these strategies work. Throughout much of my career in the corporate world, my role was to bring to life the big visions of Idea Magnets. I always paired well with them. (You might say that we were naturally attracted to each other.) They generated amazing ideas, and I figured out how to make those ideas happen.

When I left my corporate job to start The Brainzooming Group, I found myself thrust into a new leadership role. Realizing I'd now have to be more of a creative leader for our team and clients inspired me to study what the Idea Magnets I knew did to develop and sustain such creative impact. I was surprised to find their characteristics had rubbed off on me! That's when the concept of Idea Magnets was born.

In those early days of exploring Idea Magnets, it became clear that there was an entire globe of them out there. That's why building a network of Idea Magnets is even easier today, since you can make connections virtually all over the world.

To start tapping into your creative forces, join our Idea Magnet community, share your experiences, and attract more creativity to your life by following @IdeaMagnets and #IdeaMagnets on Facebook, Twitter, and Instagram.

To give yourself a boost, download *The Idea Magnets Creative Recharge*. It shares strategies that build on the ideas here and offer fun approaches to recharging creative energy. You can download it by visiting IdeaMagnets.com/recharge.

# 2

# If your Name is Brown, Why is your Color Orange?

Y ou may have noticed when you picked up this book that my name is Mike Brown. Then again, you may not have noticed. Mike Brown is an incredibly common name. The website HowManyOfMe.com estimates there are 32,000 people named Mike Brown in the U.S. alone.

Yet, if you've met me, you've probably noticed that even though my name is Brown, I'm always wearing orange. The story behind my journey to orange is really the beginning of my evolution from working with Idea Magnets to becoming one.

### Here's My Story

I'm proud that my name is Brown, but despite my saying and hearing it every day, the color has never been prominent in my life.

6

With this contradiction (being Brown, but not brown), it's no wonder I spent nearly 19 years working at a transportation company named Yellow whose brand color was orange. Somehow the contradiction escaped me for several years. Senior management didn't care for orange, so we didn't call any attention to it. Even though I was more oblivious than unaccepting of this, the result was the same.

When Greg Reid took over as the Chief Marketing Officer at Yellow, he immediately noticed the contradiction and said, "If our customers' most-asked question is 'Why is your company name Yellow if your color is orange?' then let's do something with it." We started turning everything orange, including our clothes. As a first step, the marketing staff even wore orange socks to our new strategic plan presentation.

As we boldly embraced the yellow-orange contradiction, it triggered a friendly competition between another employee and me to see who could sport the most orange. The competition included orange socks, shirts, shoes, backpacks, cups, etc. I became known for wearing orange socks daily. (Eventually the magazine *Fast Company* profiled us and called me the Cal Ripken, Jr. of orange socks, which, obviously, only strengthened the connection.)

As all the dramatic changes we were making became known, people sought me out to speak about innovation. Researching what orange represents more thoroughly, I discovered it matched my topics: creativity, innovation, and success. Taking advantage of this opportunity, I co-opted the company's brand as part of my own. Orange became *my* color. I used orange even more purposefully to link my personal brand and key themes in the content I shared.

## My Evolution...And Yours

Sometimes the creative connections that lead to great ideas take a long time. Realizing that Yellow (the company) and orange were an unusual combination took years. Similarly, making the unusual connection between orange and Brown (me) developed over a few years. At other times, creative ideas strike suddenly, through divine inspiration. That's what happened with the emergence of Brainzooming as a descriptor of the style of strategic creative thinking we'd been developing in our corporate setting when I was at Yellow.

At Yellow, we designed and facilitated hundreds of creative strategy workshops at our company's subsidiaries. Also, we tried out our emerging methodology in other settings. We did a number of these innovation workshops in partnership with John Pepper, a marketing executive and a professor at Baker University near Kansas City. One time, John asked that the students work with three creativity exercises and prioritize their ideas in a 50-minute class.

As I put the material together the Saturday before our workshop, it seemed daunting to do so much in so little time. Suddenly the thought popped in my head, "At that point, it's not even brainstorming. It's brainzooming." I stopped typing, played it back to myself and looking up, said silently, "Thank you, God!" My next stop was Google, which revealed no hits for "brainzooming." Checking the URL, I learned that Brainzooming.com was unclaimed. I said, "Thank you, God!" again, grabbed the URL, and first used the name the following Monday in class. I filed for a trademark, and there it was: I now had a brand name and a color that started attracting attention among innovators and business people.

Brainzooming—the style of creative thinking— reflects the heart of how we at The Brainzooming Group work with executives wrestling with strategy. We help them rapidly think through a smarter set of possibilities, turn strong ideas into solid strategies, and implement them for better results and success.

Attaching a name to the process we developed is just one example of cultivating a team of Idea Magnets for this new, entrepreneurial chapter in my life. While the steps to putting all the pieces together weren't *always* deliberate, they linked to my dream of surrounding people with tools and frameworks to take the chance out of developing strategy and innovative ideas.

* * *

I share my story of personal change to provide you with some background and to illustrate that we are *all* developing and growing throughout our lives. If you are thinking that there is just no way *you* are an Idea Magnet that will successfully attract other Idea Magnets, let me say one more time: you *are* and you most certainly *will*!

If it could happen for me, it can happen for you. Now let's dive in to the seven strategies that will put the charge into your Idea Magnetism!

# 3

# The Seven Strategies

There are seven strategies for cultivating your own magnetic field and attracting Idea Magnets. Let's look at each one briefly so you can start thinking through each strategy, where your strengths are, and how you and others are living these out in your personal and work lives.

1. Generating Inspiration
2. Embodying Servant Leadership
3. Attracting Opposites
4. Making Unexpected Connections
5. Encouraging People and Ideas
6. Implementing for Impact
7. Recharging Creative Energy

Here is an idea of what you'll find in each of the chapters that illustrate individual strategies.

### Generating Inspiration

Idea Magnets generate interest and passion for the big objectives and dramatic visions they create within their organizations and in their personal lives. Unlike creative geniuses who may work on a more solitary basis, Idea Magnets want strong creative leaders surrounding them. The entire team's creativity leads to imagining the details that turn bold visions into realities.

In sharing a big vision for an organization, what's important is that it boldly challenges and stretches the organization in dynamic, positive ways.

*Idea Magnets ground creative ideas in strategies and objectives. They are pursuing creativity to accomplish a significant impact.*

### Embodying Servant Leadership

Idea Magnets are servant leaders. They participate in the challenging tasks they ask their teams to address. They also grow their team members into Idea Magnets themselves through strategic mentorship, fostering collaboration, leading with strategic patience, and exhibiting true transparency.

They surround themselves with smarter, more talented people, encouraging team members to also become adept at leading and challenging the status quo while serving others.

*Idea Magnets are in the middle of imagining ideas AND accomplishing results. Rather than sitting on the sidelines for the real work of innovation, they demonstrate how doing is as important as imagining.*

### Attracting Opposites

Just as magnets attract the opposite poles of other magnets, Idea Magnets attract diverse individuals and

11

their ideas. What makes Idea Magnets so attractive? They charge the workplace and life with excitement. They take the opposite approach to conventional ways of doing things. What others would consider as limitations, they see as opportunities. They maximize the potential of physical space, time, resources, tools, and interactions with new people, leading to creative ideas and action.

*Idea Magnets know that two opposing forces can be brought together in a powerful new combination. Attracting many diverse, creative forces yields tremendous benefits.*

### Making Unexpected Connections

Idea Magnets connect people and situations to energize creativity. They are great "and" thinkers— meaning they embrace and easily work with both sides of what others might see as conflicting perspectives. Idea Magnets are strong at:

- Generating and prioritizing ideas
- Thinking creatively and implementing ideas
- Exploiting tested ideas and unknown possibilities

Using creative formulas, Idea Magnets identify possibilities and combine them in new ways to create powerful new ideas.

*Idea Magnets excel at spotting relationships between things that seem disconnected. These connections trigger innovative ideas and lead to realizing future opportunities.*

## Encouraging People and Ideas

Idea Magnets motivate team members in many ways. They routinely facilitate unique creative experiences that maximize new perspectives. They combine team members in unique combinations and invite new people into groups to freshen group dynamics. They celebrate successes and lessons learned from new ideas even when they fall short of their intended impacts.

*By adding new and unusual variables, Idea Magnets routinely facilitate unique creative experiences for their teams. This concept extends to personal relationships, where the right words and surprising settings provide powerful platforms for change!*

## Implementing for Impact

Idea Magnets imagine and attract many ideas. They embrace taking productive risks, making strategic decisions, and moving forward collaboratively. Most importantly, they foster these behaviors in their teams.

When an initiative launches, Idea Magnets focus on ensuring their teams are prepared and supported so they can best perform successfully. By providing upfront direction on how much freedom team members have to explore and experiment during implementation, they enable strong engagement and ownership.

*While they say in brainstorming sessions there are no bad ideas, you can only move ahead with a certain number of possibilities. It's vital to select the right time to decide on the strongest ideas to pursue and implement for impact.*

## Recharging Creative Energy

Applying creative thinking to business issues is mentally stimulating. There's still the need, however, for Idea Magnets to recharge creative energy for themselves and their teams. Idea Magnets understand what encourages their creative passions and what will prepare team members to maximize their creative energies.

*Managing a business team's creativity is like a basketball coach managing the varied personalities and talents on the team. The Idea Magnet has to try a variety of "player" combinations before the team scores creatively.*

Those are the seven strategies for becoming an Idea Magnet and attracting other magnets to your team. You might be wondering if an Idea Magnet's creative business thinking is important if you don't work in a creative field or company. The answer is simple and loud: Yes! It's even more important in this instance to bring fresh ideas to how an organization delivers customer value.

# 4

# Generating Inspiration

Let's throw out some of those iron filings I mentioned at the start and see how we can go to school on Idea Magnets, understand what they're doing, and better emulate their inspirational impact.

Sure, Idea Magnets are inspiring. They go *beyond* inspiring people to be slightly better or to realize an incremental gain. Idea Magnets inspire others to collaborate and accomplish purposeful, exciting, and amazing things.

How do Idea Magnets inspire themselves and those around them? First, an Idea Magnet makes make sure his or her personal core purpose is solid. This grounding in what's important extends to their teams and organizations. Idea Magnets lead the charge on important work that makes a difference by building significant initiatives on strategic foundations. By exploiting their own talents and those of the team, each team member is concentrating their energies in the areas where they have distinctive talents. As a result, imagining and implementing extreme creativity comes naturally.

How do you foster this groundswell of creativity? Once you've tapped into the source of your own creativity, exciting others to team up with bold creativity is easy. Teammates can see each other's talents (and perhaps discover additional ones), collaborating in new ways for previously unimagined ideas and successes.

Let's look at how one Idea Magnet inspired my first crazy idea as a college student; all because he helped his team believe they were destined to do amazing things!

* * *

As a child, I had fanciful ideas and imagined the great things I'd do as an adult. These aspirations focused on baseball, art, and music. Then, as happens with so many of us, once I got into organized activities, it became apparent that my aspirations outstripped my talents. I lasted a couple of years in Little League baseball before discovering there were no great fielding, weak hitting right-handed first basemen in the major leagues for a reason! Art and music aspirations lasted a bit longer because I could do those with less structure and need for official validation.

Over time, I dropped any hope of doing anything extraordinary. The official messages in my life were that I was average. In the areas where I still had a glimmer of self-confidence in my personal promise to stand out, I never connected with others having similar interests that we could explore and develop together.

Once I got to college that started to change as I began working with the first Idea Magnet of my career.

I knew the local university had started producing big name concerts. From news stories, it seemed a guy named Dave Brown was behind them. He wasn't a relative. I didn't know him at all. I knew, though, that if I wound up going to the local university, I was going to make it on the concert committee and be a part of attracting rock concerts to Hays, Kansas.

Amazingly, that's what happened. In a lackadaisical freshman year of college, my first proactive move was to apply for and earn selection to the concert committee. Shortly after meeting Dave Brown, his penchant for big, bold thinking was obvious. He created excitement throughout campus and the community. Dave had the vision of making the university's concert program the premier one in the United States despite having fewer than 5,000 students. It was easy to be inspired by this idea after Fort Hays staged a string of concerts with top rock and roll acts at the peaks of their success. Dave's big thinking inspired me to start imagining possibilities I never would have previously.

One day MTV showed that Billy Joel had an open tour date traveling from Omaha to Denver on his concert schedule. I quickly called Dave, saying we should get him to do a concert date in Western Kansas on the way. Within days, we worked up a proposal for a bigger, more expensive concert than we'd ever produced before and had the offer in front of Billy Joel's team. They said the offer was incredible. Unfortunately, Billy didn't want to work one more night on the tour.

Dave's willingness to make it all happen really did signal *anything* might be possible. Even today, decades later, people are still reminiscing about these concerts and the caliber of the performers that they would not have been able to see in Western Kansas had it not been for Dave Brown's big vision.

These college experiences revealed three important Idea Magnet lessons.

An Idea Magnet's vision embraces extreme creativity for a big purpose. They figure out the big vision and share it first. Dave's vision of making our tiny college the premier location for major concerts was known by his team and nearly everyone on campus and in the community. Working under that bold goal unleashed extreme creativity to devise strategies to realize big visions. I would have never even *had* the idea to get Billy Joel if Dave hadn't communicated his vision to us. He inspired me to look for new ways to achieve the vision along with the empowerment to do something about it.

Secondly, as rich and challenging as Dave's ambition was for the program, he left it to us to develop the strategies and ideas to pursue it. That's where the energized people an Idea Magnet attracts can imagine the sometimes wild, aspirational ideas needed to bring the visions to reality. Those are heady experiences.

Finally, Idea Magnets know not all their big visions are going to be realized. That's all part of imagining and pursuing big ideas. One common element, though, is the audacity of their visions and how everyone in the organization and its audiences needs to know an Idea Magnet is headed to someplace very different than where they had been before.

\* \* \*

## In Action: Cultivating Personal Inspiration

Despite working for and with Idea Magnets, spontaneously painting a big vision was never my strong suit. Working for Idea Magnets, I honed my skills at bringing their visions to life. With my own company, the role has changed. I've had to try mastering the best ways to articulate big visions. The moral of the story? Never assume you won't be thrust into a fully-fledged Idea Magnet role at some point in your career.

If you are inspired to become an Idea Magnet for yourself and your team, how do you make the changes necessary to bring your aspirations to life? You can begin by developing your own core purpose to serve as your personal foundation for important, creative work. Like a company might communicate the reason for its existence, a personal core purpose should be the driving force in your life that aligns all your activities.

## Finding Your Core Purpose

Identifying and articulating a core purpose whether for you personally, team members, or an organization can be straight forward. It takes more time to do the reflecting than the actual writing. Start exploring what your core purpose might be by asking and answering these questions. They will trigger ideas suited for describing your life's direction:

- What things motivate me to get out of bed every morning?
- In what ways am I of the greatest service to others?
- What brings me happiness & contentment?
- What things do I find most fulfilling?
- On what would I invest my time, talents, & attention if I didn't have to work?
- What things can I accomplish that are long-lasting and significant?
- At the end of my life, what things will make me smile when I look back?

Answering these questions will yield an abundance of ideas, beliefs, inspirations, and possibilities that could comprise your core purpose.

19

If you look at organizational core purpose statements, you quickly see a pattern for how they are stated. Examples from two major brands' original core purpose statements reveal it:

- 3M: To solve unsolved problems innovatively.
- Walmart: To give ordinary folk the chance to buy the same things as rich people

Try organizing your core purpose, when the time is right, using this simple formula:

To + [VERB] + [What? or Who?] + [How? What? or Why?]

This format structures the common themes emerging from your answers into a personal core purpose statement. Not only does the formula help you organize your thinking, it also suggests what types of words you need to use to complete your work.

Looking back at our corporate examples, 3M's formula is a VERB (solve) + WHAT (unsolved problems) + HOW (innovatively), while the Walmart core purpose is a VERB (give) + WHO (ordinary people) + WHAT (the chance to buy the same things as rich people).

You may also notice a creative tension inside the Walmart core purpose. It talks about *giving*, but Walmart is all about *selling*. Similarly, I worked for a transportation company whose core purpose verb was *making*, yet we provided a service. We didn't make anything. That creative tension isn't a must for a core purpose statement's effectiveness, yet it can be an intriguing element to include if it fits the direction that is emerging for you.

When articulating my own core purpose, I was in a period of spiritual reawakening. While my original version revolved around having a sense of financial security, I came to the realization that this ultimately meant nothing to anyone. As a result, my exploration morphed completely into stating a core purpose focused on serving others daily. Without that more fully-developed core purpose, I would never have left my corporate job to launch an entrepreneurial career that focused on helping organizations and their people engage more successfully in strategy and innovation.

With a financially-oriented core purpose, I would have hung on to a big corporation's security, paychecks, bonuses, and budgets. With a core purpose devoted to serving others, making the jump from corporate security into the uncertain, but highly-focused, opportunity of helping others be more innovative was the only thing to do! Aligning my priorities, decisions, and activities to my core purpose provides an incredible peace of mind and personal motivation. I know it can do the same for you.

As you complete your personal core purpose, electing to share it with others is a decision you'll have to make. Whether others know the exact wording of your core purpose or not, you should be living it through your actions and your priorities both in your work and personal life.

* * *

As an Idea Magnet, you need to be able to find inspiration whenever you need it.

I used to think creative inspiration came from inside.

As a result, the pressure for inspiration and creative thinking was always dependent on me. What ideas did I need to imagine? How could I trigger creative thinking? What situations could manifest desperately-needed inspiration?

21

At some point, God provided the grace to realize creative inspiration came from the outside, not the inside. While creative thinking *did* have something to do with me, it wasn't completely *dependent* on me.

Here's what I learned:

Inspiration arrives when you open yourself to answers and ideas moving about you – whether you recognize them or not. It involves being hopeful, ever watchful, and patient to see what leads to inspiration. It's being blessed to recognize and embrace signs, signals, apparent coincidences, and clues God generously offers to realize opportunities and solve problems.

There's that old saying about God helping those that help themselves. I'd change it to say God helps everyone; it's just that some people work *with* God in more open ways than others to take advantage of the help.

**Creating Your Inspiration Inventory**

Even the greatest Idea Magnets experience times when they feel stuck and need ideas right away. When your patience for creative ideas is low, you need dependable structures to trigger new thinking. To help with these situations in the future, take some time soon to complete an Inspiration Inventory when you *are* feeling creative. Later, when you need personal inspiration, you'll have your own personal creativity menu to push yourself out of the doldrums.

Grab a pen and paper (or a voice memo on your smartphone) and spend a few minutes answering these questions. If you are too busy right now, commit to spending just 10 minutes later to complete them:

- Who boosts your creative thinking?
- What situations inspire you?

- When do you feel like you're at your strongest creatively?
- Where can you go to recharge your creative thinking?
- Why does your creativity flourish when it is most abundant?
- How have you previously triggered new creative thinking when you've been stuck?

### Getting to Extreme Creativity Easily

In a store window while I was traveling with my wife Cyndi in New Orleans, a poster caught my eye. It was *Peter's Laws: The Creed of the Sociopathic Obsessive Compulsive.* These laws weren't very flattering—they were about ignoring the rules, always asking for more, and creating a challenge when you don't have one. Still, these laws explained how the Idea Magnets I had known behaved, albeit in a more socially acceptable way, when they were at the heights of their creative unconventionality.

I bought the poster thinking: If Peter's Laws shed light on how creative powerhouses approach game-changing creativity; they should yield questions *anyone* can use to push their own extreme creativity. That was the start of my quest to identify and develop new questions and structures that routinely deliver over-sized creative ideas no matter how an individual feels about his or her creative skills.

The questions I developed inspired by these laws and other case studies of individuals displaying extreme creativity are effective in getting otherwise mild-mannered, conventional individuals to become outrageously creative. And when you use them with people inclined toward wild creativity, watch out!

23

What are some of the most robust extreme creativity questions?

- What would be bigger and bolder than anything you have ever done and potentially impossible for you to pull off successfully?
- What big, new and radical things are the smartest people and organizations (regardless of industry) doing that you need to do too?
- What even more outlandish things would you do if there were no rules?
- If someone tells you "no," what are you going to do to go around or above them and keep going?
- What would you be doing if you could never hear any objections people might raise?
- What can you do to dramatically speed up every element of the big projects you are working on right now?
- What can you do that is completely opposite of anything typical or expected?
- What would you do if your goal were to be 100x bigger or more impressive than you are today?
- What will create impossible-to-ignore buzz daily about what you're doing and accomplishing?

These nine questions are simply a start. You can add to your own list in various ways. For example, you could scour stories about creative thinkers and imagine the extreme creativity questions behind their ideas. You could turn quotes from creative giants into questions and challenge yourself or your team to multiply that creativity. Suffice it to say, experience suggests that big questions will produce extreme creativity from anyone.

# In Action: Inspiring Daily Creativity in your Team Members

Typically, creative thinking exercises are a huge source of inspiration to imagine new ideas. When most people use these types of exercises, they experience rapid fire ideas and are open to generating a larger quantity of ideas rather than perfect ideas. These creative thinking exercises don't work for everyone, however. In those cases, you must be ready with alternatives to engage the innate creativity of all your team members.

### New Ideas Don't Have to be Perfect Ideas

For example, I had completed a workshop on creativity and innovation for a large volunteer organization. From the energy in the room and attendees' comments, it seemed a success. For one attendee, though, there was tremendous discomfort. She told me she was creative in other areas on her own time, by herself. Or she could express creativity when she patterned what she did creatively on someone else's approach. While she wanted to contribute to the group's creative thinking exercises, she "froze up" when she was "put on the spot."

I told my new friend that she was just like I had been. And, I can still be the person that doesn't want to mess up a creative idea right from the start or expend creative energy on things I don't think will lead to success or progress.

To help her begin to break through this roadblock, I bought her a cheap sketchbook (not a nicely bound book that says, "Don't mess up a page" to someone like her), a few Sharpies, and a couple of the Pilot pens I use to scribble notes. Inside the sketch book, I wrote this message for her.

This isn't a book for good ideas or bad ideas. It's a place to put "getting started" ideas or inspirations or possibilities. It isn't about perfection. It's all about dreaming, trying, and learning what new creativity you'll bring to life...even if no one else ever sees it!!!

Beyond the book, we discussed ways to lower the stakes in imagining and doing something with new creative ideas. These included getting okay with ideas that only progress a small amount, exploring concepts that are completely changeable, and simply forcing yourself to share ideas that are uncomfortable to you, but could make sense to others.

You will work with individuals during your career (or maybe it is you) who struggle with generating ideas because they want them to be right before they do anything with them, or even before they share them with others. To inspire creativity in team members laboring under this burden, make sure they feel safe to have and communicate what seem like lousy ideas.

To start, let your employees know that you understand that ideas are born out of imagining, then trying and learning, and finally making changes. Don't tell them this once. Make it part of your organization's culture. And lead by example—don't be afraid to share your less-than-stellar ideas as you have them. That helps dispel the sense that you only have good ideas!

## Overcoming Your Team's Creative Roadblocks

Most, dare I say all, organizations would benefit from bigger and bolder ideas, but the reality is that these ideas can be elusive.

Asking people for big ideas isn't the answer. Asking *big questions* is the key. Using the same extreme creativity questions you use to trigger your own inspiration is a fantastic strategy to cultivate extreme breakthrough ideas in a group, also. This helps to break the temptation for others to sit back and wait for you to share your unbelievable ideas. It is also an ideal way to attract others to your vision, bringing them along the path to being Idea Magnets themselves.

Still, some teams get paralyzed when they need to think creatively. They may be stuck believing that they need to be in exactly the right mental state to start. Or they're waiting for inspiration or the right set of conditions before attempting creative thinking.

One way to address this paralysis is to decide upfront that the team can automatically discard anything created in the initiative's first hours if it isn't ultimately productive or on track. A willingness to throw away early work can get the team moving beyond initial hesitancies.

If your aspiration for big ideas is about volume rather than the size of ideas, get more people concurrently generating ideas. One way is to fill a room with paper and markers. Break into small groups where many people can actively participate at the same time. This will stretch individual imaginations and expand the number of creative ideas. Encourage people to doodle ideas using pictures if that works better than words for them. The doodles need not be perfect or well-drawn; they just serve as another way to communicate team member thinking.

Another way to take advantage of the same formula (more people participating concurrently with highly productive thinking exercises) is to have a group collaborate virtually. In that case, you can have every team member participating all at once even if they are in multiple locations.

No matter the approach you take, the key to gaining the advantage from generating lots of ideas is to make sure they are all captured. By recording all the ideas that are shared, individuals and the group overall can express their preferences for ideas possessing the most opportunity.

From this treasure trove of collaborative input, you can develop intriguing concepts and strategies. This approach also inspires people to participate the next time you need them to engage in strategic thinking.

## Keep Team Members on Track

Team members may apologize for making suggestions by saying, "This doesn't fit the question, but here's an idea."

Even though creative thinking exercises are intended to help people approach familiar situations in new ways, they can constrain thinking. When people become so focused on answering *only* the creative thinking target, they may self-censor ideas not directly addressing the question. When this happens, creative exercises that should free up thinking can become boxes that close off ideas.

Always explain to a group that creative thinking questions and strategic thinking exercises are simply *starting points* to launch new ideas. They should inspire, not limit, thinking. Someone thinking creatively should not have to justify a new idea that seems to come from nowhere. Likewise, other group members shouldn't use creative thinking questions as a club to beat down a new idea because it appears off track in relation to what the group is addressing that minute. With all the roadblocks to new thinking that float around us all the time, the last thing you ever want to happen is for a creative thinking question to morph into one more "no" to new ideas.

* * *

Idea Magnets cultivate dynamic visions and objectives that point in dramatically new directions. They excel at pushing people to be their unimagined best. Even when an Idea Magnet's vision seems impossible, ridiculous, or nonsensical to others, the inspiration itself remains grounded in the overall strategy.

# 5

# Embodying Servant Leadership

While Idea Magnets have egos, they build trust within their teams by *doing* what they say. They display vulnerability, honesty, humility, and high ethical standards. They are servant leaders.

At the heart of servant leadership is the idea that those who seek to lead must serve. And since all of us can serve one another, leadership is open to everyone. This is why Idea Magnets place a high priority on effectively developing leaders within their teams.

### Leading, Doing, and Supporting

Individuals with a propensity toward servant leadership instinctively look at opportunities and issues with others' interests as the starting perspective.

You might think that a servant leader is always in the background. That isn't accurate, though. Sometimes a servant leader is putting a teammate in the position to be in front and in charge; at other times, the servant leader must be in the spotlight when that's what it takes for the team to succeed.

Servant leadership is a fascinating concept, particularly for those who feel as if they don't get rewarded with workplace promotions that they "rightly" deserve.

Servant leaders display an unselfish, team-oriented mentality. This attitude is sometimes demonstrated by assisting others to make sure they take on difficult situations without the servant leader stepping in to fix things. These situations are sometimes painful for a team member, but they are a vital part of learning.

### Don't Be the Smartest Person in the Room

I have worked with multiple leaders who operate from a position of insecurity. They know they have holes in their leadership skills—all leaders do. Instead of addressing their personal weaknesses by surrounding themselves with others who have strengths in those areas, they try to mask their weaknesses through an overly-aggressive style. They must be right. They must be the ones in the spotlight. They must be the smartest people on their teams.

These types of leaders are not Idea Magnets.

You see, when people think you are the smartest person in the room, all the responsibility is on you. Who else is going to come up with the best ideas, the most insightful analysis, the most stirring comments?

Nobody. How could they be expected to do it when you're the best?

An Idea Magnet knows that one important way to display servant leadership, and to actively cultivate it within a team, is conveying the message that they can learn from everyone.

31

I discovered that idea as a child from an unlikely source: the TV show *All in the Family*. Actor Richard Masur played a mentally challenged grocery store delivery person that Archie Bunker, the curmudgeonly main character, didn't trust because he was different. After an unpleasant exchange, the young man disappeared, only to return with a framed quote that was tremendously important to him: "Every man is my superior in that I may learn from him."

It's amazing how specific instances stick with you for years. That childhood memory profoundly shaped my thinking ever since. Googling the quote now provides mixed opinions on whether it is from Ralph Waldo Emerson or Thomas Carlyle. Either way, it is forever linked to that program for me. Its impact led to the realization that I'm the lesser of every person that I meet and that I need to understand what I should learn from them.

\* \* \*

To further your idea magnetism, surround yourself with people who are smart, creative, and dynamic. Ask a few questions and let your team members contribute their own perspectives. Building from others' ideas cultivates a robust sense of participation and ownership.

And guess what?

Not only will you get better answers and results, you can sit back and get smarter by learning from your team! Embrace bringing people who are better and smarter than you onto your team.

Doing so:

- Creates better results.
- Continually challenges your team and disrupts the status quo.

32

- Let other team members learn from people who are better than them.
- Makes everyone on the team better at their roles within the team.

Getting comfortable surrounding yourself with more talented team members can be a struggle. I understand. It has also been a challenge for me. Not because I'm afraid of smarter and better people, but because I labor under the belief that those folks would have little interest in having me contributing around them. If you also struggle with this belief, I challenge you to find the smartest, most creative and dynamic person either at your company or that you know in a volunteer role and ask to work with them. Chances are they'll be thrilled by your request.

### Mentoring Your Team

One way Idea Magnets serve others is through active mentorship. Idea Magnets need to develop extended teams to carry out the strategies and ideas that bring vision to reality. This allows them to make the greatest impact by expanding their vision and getting support from individuals who have strengths in other areas. It speeds the process, too, because, after all, there is only so much time in the day.

Idea Magnets should also seek out mentors, even if the relationships are relatively informal. Different mentors fill different development needs, so you will need different mentors at various points in your career.

Despite potentially varied roles, all mentors should:
- Provide an experienced point of view.
- Expand and shape your professional perspectives and learning.

- Help prioritize and develop your talents to realize your career objectives.
- Constructively challenge you based on an objective view of your situation.

How do Idea Magnets grow their impact as servant leaders and mentors for their teams? How do they develop as strong collaborative leaders? The remainder of this chapter provides activities you can practice for yourself as well as introduce within your team.

\* \* \*

## In Action: Being an Effective Collaborative Leader

To develop trust and respect within their teams, servant leaders advocate and practice collaboration with team members whenever possible. Use this list to gauge your own readiness to act as a collaborative leader for your team, asking yourself, what are my strengths in:

- Perceiving and sharing strong insights?
- Growing the diversity of my experience?
- Gaining knowledge across multiple fields?
- Asking robust, probing questions?
- Accommodating new thinking and perspectives?
- Sorting through details to isolate critical issues?
- Challenging my personal perspectives?
- Being okay with productive disagreements that lead to better results?

Reviewing this checklist will help cultivate your readiness and allow you to see the areas where you need to grow as a collaborative, servant-oriented leader.

## Vital Behaviors of Collaborative Strategy Leaders

Sometimes collaborative leadership doesn't come naturally. In some companies, where performance measures place an emphasis on personal (versus team) results, there are few incentives to develop collaborative leadership skills. Even at these companies, however, strong collaborative leaders are present. My company, The Brainzooming Group, has worked with these individuals across industries. Despite the differences in industries and organizations, we find collaborative leaders demonstrating a common set of behaviors that parallel those of Idea Magnets.

### They actively seek out organizational energy.

Collaborative leaders continually reach out in all directions to learn what people in the organization are passionate about and trying to make happen. They connect with people up, down, and across the organization. They reach out to all levels and areas to ask questions, listen, synthesize what they learn, and share updates back to their own teams and others integral to team and organization success.

### They integrate the organization's energy and activities into collaborative ideas and strategies.

When a collaborative leader sees activities even remotely linked to bigger organizational aspirations, they work to integrate them. That means finding points of connection and offering or suggesting adjustments that align activities to overarching strategies to accelerate momentum.

They connect the people that will benefit each other.

Idea Magnets connect the people that are pursuing related activities or whose varied talents and experiences will benefit each other. Creating these connections helps an organization move forward more quickly and dramatically with greater alignment.

They serve the people, the collaborative initiatives, and the organization above their own concerns.

This is the foundation of a servant-oriented, collaborative leadership style. Collaborative leaders are motivated to act based on the overall good instead of what suits their own agendas or even their parts of organizations. They are leading collaborative strategy for their organization's overall successes—even if it means ignoring their own interests to benefit the team.

### Patient Leadership

Exercising *strategic patience*—the conscious decision to pause, delay, or take extra time to consider outcomes and implications—can appear to be laziness, inattentiveness, or indifference. And what leader wants to be associated with those characteristics?

The fact is that we expect leaders to act because action is tangible. Action implies one's ability to fix something and check a problem off a list, even if the issue may require work beyond what's on a to-do list. The easy move when a problem confronts a leader is to act immediately. You won't find many people who will argue with, "I did something about that right away!"

An Idea Magnet, to the contrary, *must* both push for action and exercise strategic patience with team members. Idea Magnets see ahead of others. Yet, they need to exhibit patience as others strive to better

36

understand the vision and strategies that an Idea Magnet has already foreseen. Thus, strategic patience goes hand-in-hand with serving your team as a leader and being an effective mentor—even though patience can be one of the toughest behaviors to practice.

Some examples of exercising strategic patience in the workplace include:

- Taking more time than expected to explore new thinking and try different methods
- Accepting the idiosyncrasies that team members may bring to creative pursuits
- Understanding mistakes will inevitably happen, thereby extending the time to learn and recover
- Being flexible to redirections and changes in course to get to the objective
- Waiting for answers that may not materialize right away

While Idea Magnets need to exercise patience strategically, they also need to be careful to not let opportunities that are paused disappear. An Idea Magnet strikes the right balance between waiting and advancing by monitoring indicators to see when it is time to act and involving team members who naturally instigate for action. While I cannot put a specific percentage on the number of times strategic patience will work more effectively than acting right away, I have found it to be significant in my career. And, the success rate of strategic patience seems to be getting higher as people's stress levels lead to more perceived problems and less inclination to wait and think before acting.

### Be Transparent, Truly Transparent

A church I regularly attend received a new pastor, replacing another relatively new pastor. It was a bit of a mystery why the previous pastor left, leading to an information void. That prompted speculation about what was going on and what would happen next. This speculation extended to the new priest, who seemed to have issues in his past, based on an online search.

When it came time for the homily at the new pastor's first service, he said the bishop told him to share his whole story that weekend so there would be no questions.

He explained his unwillingness in the early years of his priesthood to say no to any new assignment. He took on additional parishes, achieved big goals, and over-extended himself. Through whatever factors, he came to abuse alcohol and, as he stated, "compromised his values." When the situation became known several years ago, the bishop pushed him to disclose everything. The bishop then called the media to ensure there was no hint of anything being concealed.

The priest discussed hitting rock bottom that day, and the steps he had taken since to get back on his feet. In the "recovery community," he surrounds himself with people to foster accountability. He acknowledged moderating his previous ambitions.

He tied the entire message together with the theme for the feast of All Saints Day by reminding us "every saint has a past, and every sinner has a future."

Importantly, his message was not an apology for being caught. It was an admission of falling and working hard to get back up.

When he concluded, he was greeted by warm applause from the congregation—a very rare occurrence at a Roman Catholic mass.

The new pastor's emphasis on immediately sharing the entire story with his new flock was a lesson in what real transparency looks like.

With it, he:

- Let everyone know that he, like all the rest of us, needs help to grow and improve.
- Fostered a willingness among parishioners to be supportive in his recovery.
- Signaled to parishioners in the recovery community that he was someone to reach out to if they need support.
- Perhaps most importantly, any rumormongers were put out of business day one since we all learned the truth at the same time.

* * *

The term "transparency" is thrown around a lot even though it is carried out less frequently.

Idea Magnets practice real transparency similar to the way this pastor did. It is critical to building the trust they need to share bold strategies and engage enthusiasm and hard work on ideas team members may not initially understand.

Contrast what real transparency looks like with the transparency many public figures represent. When famous people are caught compromising their values, they typically apologize for getting caught, without ever acknowledging they did anything wrong. This faux transparency cultivates distrust and skepticism since the whole apologizing for getting caught routine is too scripted and insincere.

Being an effective Idea Magnet requires true transparency—including clearly sharing your ambitions as well as your mistakes.

# In Action: Developing Team Members into Collaborative, Servant-Oriented Leaders

An Idea Magnet is always thinking about fostering a community of collaborative, servant-oriented leadership within his or her team. Since Idea Magnets make sure there are many other smart people around, they must find the right balance between sharing the big vision and dictating too many details on how they expect it to play out during implementation.

To pave the way toward finding that balance and creating an environment for team leadership and success, I teach this checklist in strategic thinking workshops.

Idea Magnets need to:

- State objectives, not details, so team members have an opportunity to shape implementation.
- Share what they know or suspect while making room for team members to bring new insights and thinking to the vision.
- Allow leaders to be owners as they develop their own skills as Idea Magnets.
- Listen to ideas and provide timely responses so team members aren't left waiting for input.
- Make sure they don't second guess themselves or the independent decisions team members make.
- Decide once, not twice, to place an emphasis on living with important decisions and finding ways to make them work.

This checklist provides the backdrop for bringing other talented people into your work and cultivating their growth as Idea Magnets. This approach will have you sharing the vision and objectives you're working toward while providing ample opportunities for team members to exercise their own creativity.

*  *  *

There's no specific answer for how much information sharing is too much or too little. If too much information sharing seems like it will limit your team's creativity and investment in the project, you're better off under-sharing what you know.

Transfer some (or even all) of the ownership on initiatives to your team members. This provides opportunities for them to shape the group's important work. Bring them in early enough to truly shine as they share their expertise. If you wait and try to move things further along first, you risk creating a frustrating situation for everyone.

As you listen to new ideas, consider and respond to them on a timely basis, building on what has already been shared with you. Stay away from second guessing yourself *and* your team members so you're not creating a moving target for what your expectations are as you progress closer to the big vision.

### Serving Your Way to Strong Strategic Leadership

Idea Magnets are strategic at heart. They deliberately focus on the big items that matter most for organizational success. Because strategy should shape an organization's actions at all levels, bold distinctions between strategic and tactical people are ill-advised. The contrasts are mutually perpetuated by "strategic thinking" people who want to seem "important" and by "tactical, action-oriented" people who don't want to expend the mental energy (or give up their decision-making freedom) to do strategic thinking and connect their activities to an overarching business purpose.

For me, strategic thinking and tactical implementation are forever linked in successful organizations. Strategy is the connecting principle that ties tactics together. Tactics are necessary to successfully carry out a strategy.

As a result, neither strategies nor tactics can be successful without the other. Business people must maximize their contributions and successes, paying attention to both.

I'm frequently asked how to be a stronger strategic leader. When people ask this, I suspect they are looking for advice on how to be deeper thinkers and emulate C-level executives on their way to getting a bigger audience and more money. If that is the case, they are in for a big surprise when my most valuable advice for being more strategic involves the vital connection between strategy and tactics. In fact, the advice centers on behaviors that seem tactical and are rooted in servant leadership.

I tell them that one way to demonstrate real strategic leadership is to do the meeting and project tasks most co-workers avoid because they seem like low-level duties.

These involve:

- Showing up at a meeting with a proposed agenda, suggested topics, and/or relevant information. Often even the person calling the meeting isn't properly prepared to lead it. By performing these tasks, an individual will end up setting the meeting's direction and may ultimately end up steering the overall project's direction.
- Raising your hand to lead the analytical portion of an initiative. This can be more challenging and

more work, but taking the lead on identifying and delivering insights is an outstanding way to shape strategic progress and direction.

- Volunteering to develop a draft hypothesis or a business model. While this can be very involved, framing a starting hypothesis or model allows you to influence overall thinking and implementation on a strategic initiative.

Doing a fantastic job on any of these apparently tactical activities will start to make your co-workers view your business contributions in a new, different, and more strategic light. Yes, honing your meeting planning, analysis, and recommendation writing skills may not, at first look, seem the key to strategic leadership. Trust me, though: all these servant tasks are hugely strategic.

### Encouraging Your Team to Serve and Lead You

Idea Magnets are smart and effective mentors. They can still learn a tremendous amount from the perspectives of more junior team members, though. Managing upward in a mentor-mentee relationship can be tricky, even if it is exactly what an Idea Magnet needs for greater success. Doing so involves making sure those around them know and trust that the Idea Magnet is open to constructive, upward relationship management from the team. A mentee must be confident in privately challenging a misstep an Idea Magnet is making or even simply considering.

The personal trust levels required within an Idea Magnet's team are significant. You need to trust that each person will act with complete integrity both individually and as a team member. Depending on how you view trust, it can take time—at least months, if not a year or more—to develop trust based on each of you seeing a track record of the other behaving appropriately in difficult situations.

### Handle Things

An Idea Magnet's team should help him or her manage their own weaknesses. One Idea Magnet was invariably late for meetings. People would ask why I'd show up early if I knew he would be late. Being there ahead of time, however, allowed me to check the situation, smooth things over with people frustrated by his tardiness, and alert him to issues before he arrived.

While each Idea Magnet is different, playing the role of handler, especially relative to his or her weak spots, is an important aspect of helping the team succeed.

### Leading in or out of the Spotlight

Idea Magnets also need to cultivate an appreciation among team members for fulfilling what might be characterized as an understudy role to the Idea Magnet. Another way to describe it is that the team members surrounding an Idea Magnet are Idea Magnets in development. In this role, a team member may be working like crazy outside of the spotlight. While that can be a source of frustration, these times provide an important development opportunity. As someone who played the understudy role in multiple situations for many years, I can personally vouch for the advantage these critical opportunities provide to uniquely contribute and grow.

You might think someone understudying an Idea Magnet lacks the confidence to become an Idea Magnet. It's more accurate to think of them as actively developing the skills and talents of an Idea Magnet. An individual in this role needs confidence to work with a strong personality without feeling overshadowed. It's not about ratifying and cheerleading for everything the leader is trying to change.

With the leader in the spotlight, even representing work others have poured their souls into, an Idea Magnet understudy must be okay with a background role, or a lot of disappointment awaits. Still, if you have a generous boss (as I did), you are likely to be thrust into the spotlight when the time is right.

One way for an understudy to uniquely use the time outside the spotlight is by acting as additional ears and eyes for your Idea Magnet. An Idea Magnet's understudy who is actively cultivating relationships throughout the organization will regularly see, hear, and learn things the Idea Magnet never will. Sharing this information keeps the entire team smart and prepared for opportunities and challenges on the horizon and brings vital importance to the role.

### Become a Strong Interpreter

A team member should be able to translate the Idea Magnet's strategies and ideas for others. This is especially important if the Idea Magnet is new to an organization. An Idea Magnet pushing for dramatic innovation and change will make people nervous. A team member's ability to carry the change message and translate the intent the boss is targeting paves the way for greater receptivity to change.

For one Idea Magnet I worked with, I frequently had a stream of people in my office wondering what he was up to and how he thought. Being a credible and reliable source to translate the message for those who needed the help fostered valuable relationships for our team.

## Doing the Serving, Doing the Leading

There is a Chick-fil-A outdoor advertisement depicting two cows painting the fast food brand's advertising (and bovine self-preservation message) on the importance of eating more chicken. One cow is doing the painting as it stands on the other cow's back to reach the area that needs to feature the message.

When I talk about servant leadership in presentations, I generally use a picture of that billboard. For me, it does an outstanding job of demonstrating servant leadership.

Here's how:

There are two cows: one to do the writing, and one to be the ladder. Maybe they decided based on talents. Maybe they decided based on who did what last. Maybe they naturally migrated to their specific roles. No matter how they chose, each did its part to make the whole effort successful. One got to shine; one had to provide the backbone.

For me, that's what servant leadership is all about for an Idea Magnet. You may get more attention, but it doesn't have to be all the time.

One of the most important things you do as an Idea Magnet is to make sure your team knows that you are willing to be the support person, too. Strong Idea Magnets spend considerable time thinking about how to hand team members the paint brush. When team members take over, they learn, develop, and appreciate the importance of serving, along with the preciousness and fleeting nature of the spotlight.

# 6
# Attracting Opposites

Opposites attract. Read anything on magnets, and it will tell you that putting opposite poles of two strong magnets together will make them snap tight. Place the like poles close together, and they will repel—push away—from each other.

Idea Magnets take advantage of this concept. They attract the people, resources, environments, and possibilities they need to achieve incredible creativity by doing things in opposite ways from what conventional business wisdom suggests.

Executives traditionally view business as a zero-sum game; resources are fixed and a win for someone else is a loss for you. Instead of clinging to personal ownership and hoarding credit for success, however, an Idea Magnet shares the spotlight. Instead of focusing on limited resources or bogging down on self-imposed constraints, Idea Magnets attract *more* possibilities, renewable or growing resources, and look for ways for everyone to emerge as winners.

An Idea Magnet uses an *opposites attract* approach to create greater excitement for his or her team to generate more ideas and mentor up-and-coming Idea Magnets.

Idea Magnets win by sharing abundance when the popular strategy is to narrow horizons, get by with just enough resources, and seize the credit for scratching out meager success.

* * *

### Securing Mega-Space and Participation

When we were friends in college, my now-wife, Cyndi, was the first person to tell me, "White space sells." She was sharing the perspective from her public relations and journalism classes. It turns out that this deceptively simple phrase is true not only in design but also in many other areas. Ample white space is at the heart of simplifying things. It helps showcase and focus attention on the most important elements. It removes unnecessary elements fighting for attention. It makes it easier for others to process and recall what you are trying to convey.

Extending *white space sells* beyond design translates it into multiple other forms. Space may represent time, physical surroundings, silence, freedom, unfamiliarity, or any other contrasting characteristic providing room to focus and explore. Successful Idea Magnets are masters at deliberately creating more of these alternative white spaces to experiment, learn, and change.

Perhaps most frequently, Idea Magnets manage space and time to help their teams spread out and think. This helps team members to try new things. Idea Magnets do this by asking for and expecting more of what will help their teams perform successfully. They don't settle. They negotiate, push, and manage for more because they know that abundance thinking is outside of the norm.

Pushing for abundance may disaffect those responsible for delivering it. This is especially true when they would prefer to operate with a scarcity mindset. That's where an Idea Magnet balances pushiness with another area ripe for abundance: likeability. They realize they can use the following variables without limits to attract others to help accomplish their objectives by:

- Being comfortable with themselves
- Possessing a sense of wonder
- Showing interest in many things
- Radiating energy and a positive spirit
- Keeping an open mind
- Expressing self-deprecating humor
- Smiling
- Being happy to see others
- Sharing nice things about others they might not even realize
- Listening intently
- Laughing readily
- Supporting others without calling attention to it

### Attracting Too Many Ideas

I'm always surprised when an executive looking for new ideas is satisfied coming up with just a few of them. This may come from a scarcity perspective: it takes too much time to come up with ideas; it is too involved to work through a bunch of ideas; we only need one idea to be a winner, so why come up with ideas the team will never use?

In contrast, Idea Magnets know that generating ideas is easy and low-risk. It's all the other things involved in turning ideas into business successes that introduce the challenge and risk. Within that framework, why pass up the opportunity to generate more ideas than expected to find the absolute winning idea? If there is a clear winner, that's fantastic. In all likelihood, the winning idea will come from parts and pieces of multiple other ideas that surface only through accepting an abundance of ideas.

Generating ideas is a numbers game. Over the years, we have learned that 8 to 15 percent of ideas a group generates have near-term viability. That means you may need 10x or more ideas to arrive at one idea that will work. Interestingly, I heard a programming executive at ABC discuss the television network's process for developing new television series. The network's numbers were strikingly similar. From the TV show pitches and preliminary scripts it reviews in one year, ABC ordered full scripts for just over fifteen percent of the ideas. The percentage of ideas that turned into TV series that lasted more than one season? Just 0.7 percent.

Yes, Idea Magnets are constantly seeking new ideas, more ideas, and variations on ideas that already exist. They are working the ideas numbers game to keep the flow of new possibilities active and robust.

### Sharing the Creative Challenges and the Credit

An Idea Magnet knowing that he or she isn't the smartest person in the room lends itself to a particular style of team interaction.

They ask a few rich questions and let the team contribute their perspectives. Building on their ideas provides a strong sense of participation and ownership throughout the team. It also leads to better answers as well as better results. An Idea Magnet gets smarter by learning from the team.

As a bonus, the type of all-in collaborative participation blends everyone's creative contributions. Later, this makes it difficult to identify specific individuals that contributed certain parts of the final work. Everyone has a hand in the final product.

## Trusting Unconventional Ideas

One Idea Magnet stands out in my career for having the most significant impact in shaping my creative perspective and developing an appreciation for trying to attract opposites.

Coming from a consumer marketing background, Greg Reid joined Yellow Corporation (a business-to-business transportation company) as the CMO during a major turnaround. Everything was topsy-turvy. He added to it with a different mode of extreme creativity than any of those on his team had previously encountered.

He was the archetypical Idea Magnet. Of anyone on his direct team, I was the one who "got" his creative ideas and turned many of them into reality. We worked well together almost immediately—though I admit I was initially skeptical at some of Greg's wildly creative ideas.

Six months after arriving, he wanted to fly the entire corporate and field marketing and sales team to Phoenix for a kickoff meeting and retreat at a golf resort. As part of the event, he hired Earl Monroe, the former New York Knicks superstar, to speak and do a meet and greet with our internal team.

The whole thing smelled like a boondoggle *way* beyond the boundaries of acceptability at our extremely cost-conscious company. I figured the field VPs and our senior management would be in an uproar when they discovered the meeting location and planned activities.

I was *completely* wrong. The event was fantastic. The field people were excited they were included and could share their perspectives. The experience created a strong bond among all attendees. And no one in senior management said a word about the cost! (The fact we held it in Phoenix in June when the temperatures were higher than the room rates likely helped.) Greg pretty much had my complete trust in his creative instincts at that point.

So how long does it take for people to trust an Idea Magnet's unconventional way of approaching opportunities and challenges?

In my case, it took a tangible example of extreme creativity that I doubted resulting in fabulous success. Greg painted a big vision of extreme creativity I thought would fail. Ultimately, it unfolded exactly as he predicted.

After that, he had me; I was compelled to suspend any doubts about his future surprising, gigantic ideas that didn't square with my sensibilities.

When an Idea Magnet reaches that point with team members, he or she can begin aggressively taking the team toward more dramatic and amazing places.

\* \* \*

## In Action: Becoming the Opposite Force that Attracts

When you implement a strategy that runs counter to conventional wisdom—even if the world SAYS it's smart to do—prepare for criticism.

Experts celebrate failure as a vital step toward innovation. The dirty little secret is that when you're actively failing, failure SUCKS. You won't have many collaborators wanting to hang out around your extended failure, no matter what the latest innovation bestseller suggests.

Yes, Idea Magnets, you're going to need courage, faith in your instincts, and the right collaborators around you when times are more challenging than successful.

Collaboration is central to generating winning ideas, whether the collaboration is physical, virtual, or in some other form. While collaboration is important for identifying innovative ideas, not just any group of people will be successful at generating them. It's important to know who to surround yourself with, to imagine the best innovative ideas. Assembling the right team is much like a basketball coach who rotates players to find the best combination to put on the court at any one time.

To build a talented team with the greatest depth and potential for strategic and creative collaboration, use these criteria to assess how collaborative a team member might be. Team members should:

- Share similar core business values to those shaping the team.
- Bring something different (and complementary) to the team's other talents and capabilities.
- Demonstrate motivation to invest in making the collaboration as successful as possible.
- Be enthusiastic about the possibilities from collaborating.
- Display a commitment to mutual learning and benefits from collaboration.

When extending a collaborative group outside your team or organization, the upfront expectations will grow. When you expand in this direction, use these additional checkpoints:

- Find a partner that makes strategic sense and won't distract from important goals.

- Identify clear ways the parties can be of help to one another.
- Use a collaborative approach that helps both parties grow and achieve new objectives.
- Have both parties share the investment and work to make the collaboration successful, even if the types of investment are markedly different.
- Ensure both parties are comfortable equally contributing toward the strategy and ideas.
- Create a clear opportunity to learn about each other and the company (or companies) overall.
- Structure the relationship so it doesn't carry major exit costs if the results fall short.

Whether through these checkpoints or others, formalizing what you seek in collaborators is valuable in managing the size and composition of your team.

### Seeing Things Differently

Typical business wisdom suggests the smartest and most experienced people are always best suited to identify opportunities for innovation. Yet that can be a detrimental idea. For example, being too close can make a situation look very diverse when it isn't. This happens when experts rely on their uber-focused knowledge to notice differences no one else will ever perceive. The opposite challenge is that an expert's familiarity breeds blindness. In these cases, expertise overshadows the subtle differences that a neophyte notices immediately.

### Discovering What You Don't Know

If you are an expert and looking to freshen your thinking, what are viable options to highlight what you are missing?

First, keep the knowledge that you don't know everything you need to know front and center in your mind. Then, take advantage of surrounding yourself with diverse individuals who have different interests. Intently absorb the perceptions and ideas they express. Make sure the team includes individuals who will always talk with you honestly, even in difficult situations, and readily challenge your thinking. If topics where you need input are sensitive, consider letting them express their perspectives anonymously.

Take every opportunity to observe your situation from new perspectives. When you look at something very closely, maybe because you have responsibility for it, you need dependable ways to see it from blatantly different viewpoints. Strategies for this include:

Standing Further Away
- Have someone completely unfamiliar with your situation observe it, and ask them, "What are your impressions of what took place?"
- Change your seat—physically or virtually—and take a few steps back from where you usually "sit" while viewing the situation. What do you see differently?

Looking Closer
- Look at only one aspect of a process – repeat "how" and "why" questions (i.e., How is this working? Why does this happen?) until you've explored many possibilities for insights.
- Focus on the before or the after. Who do we inherit inputs from? Or who receives the output we create?

Examining Things from a Different Height

- Spend a day on the front lines with sales, manufacturing, or customer service: What do they see about a business process or opportunity that you don't?
- Spend time directly with a customer as they interact with your business: How does it look to them?
- Shadow a senior executive (maybe a mentor). What regularly makes its way to that level?

Taking a Different Perspective

- Have someone else carry out a process. What's different?
- Look from the side. Find someone with fewer ties and less wrapped up in a situation than you are and solicit their viewpoints.
- Ask someone completely unrelated—someone who has no stake in the situation—what they see.

## Stepping into New Situations with Impact

The opposite of having too much knowledge is being expected to generate high-impact ideas when you lack exposure and experience. This is familiar territory for Idea Magnets. Other leaders routinely seek them out because of how they deliver plentiful ideas and possibilities.

When you're growing as an Idea Magnet, you may be hesitant about being expected, or even approached, to step into unfamiliar situations and contribute innovative ideas right away. There are simple ways to ground your ideas and increase the value you deliver, even when you aren't schooled in a topic.

Step one is doing cursory homework upfront, concentrating on mining information sources others haven't yet explored. Coupled with reaching out to those closer to the situation for their perspectives, you can develop a framework for how you are beginning to think about the new situation. Capture your initial ideas and look for analogous situations where you have stronger experience. Take advantage of strong analogies and comparable situations to develop more ideas. Finally, never hesitate to answer a question someone poses to you by asking a question of your own to seek clarification. Asking questions doesn't convey weakness; it creates learning opportunities that increase your future impact.

### Extending Brainstorming to Daily Business

Most business people are familiar with the unique ground rules for brainstorming, such as any topic being okay for discussion and "no idea is a bad idea." Then when you return to the regular work setting, those rules go away. We prohibit certain topics and challenge ideas like crazy when we think they are...well, crazy.

What about taking an unexpected approach and employing brainstorming ground rules more broadly?

To support greater creativity in your workplace, extend typical brainstorming ground rules into everyday business life.

Your willingness to consider observations on unexpected, and even unwelcome, topics in your daily business life will foster a stronger, more creative team and organization.

This openness isn't without challenges though, particularly with people whose personal agendas get in the way. As a leader, you can still manage the less productive open discussions you may encounter. Here are some examples:

## When Something Doesn't Matter

Business people spend considerable time discussing topics with little significant impact on business results. This happens when someone gets stuck on a topic dear to them, but of little broader relevance. By actively managing discussions on marginal subjects, you send the expectation that you focus on things that drive results. As a leader, it's important to give some consideration to less prominent topics, especially if critical team members are raising them. Constrain those discussions, however, with timing appropriate to the topic's importance. You'll more than make up for what seems like wasted time by cultivating a more engaged team.

## Tackling Things That Matter a Lot

Maybe it's a strategic decision, a company's values, or an ethical principle. When a topic matters a lot, determining how open it should be for ongoing discussion is challenging. Maybe a decision has already been made or there is little appetite for discussion or debate. Yet, critical topics, when left untouched for extended periods, create blind spots. One way to allow conversation on seemingly unchangeable topics is through defined periods where they are open for discussion. This could be in conjunction with annual planning (with consideration of a company's values, vision, or strategic foundations) or during a specific forum (i.e., a special meeting or conference) where discussion is entertained and deliverables expected. Opening windows for conversation on these topics can create impactful insights without revisiting them weekly.

<u>Handling Biased Points of View</u>

I've dealt with co-workers so convinced of their own correctness that discussions on sensitive topics quickly turned unproductive. They expect their desired resolution and orient their statements toward a personal viewpoint without considering others' legitimate perspectives. In these cases, expect that "one who comes into discussion must come with clean hands."

This means an individual must enter a conversation honestly—intellectually and ethically—and be open to considering alternative positions. If someone expects to discuss an issue, yet is unwilling to consider alternative options or rethink a personal position, that person hasn't earned the opportunity for conversation. Let them know upfront that they must be ready for an open conversation, or no conversation will happen.

Opening your workplace daily to brainstorming rules isn't the norm. Yet, adopting this strategy demonstrates an Idea Magnet is truly seeking new perspectives and possibilities—even difficult ones—as they emerge in real time.

# In Action: Attracting Many Ideas

I regularly hear executives say the time their organizations spend considering new ideas is unsuccessful. They are looking for "the next big idea," and it never materializes. That creates disappointment, frustration, and a resistance to spend time considering potentially innovative ideas.

My response is always to expect that the next big idea will be elusive when that aspiration is wrapped into a meeting title and objective. Putting the phrase "next big" in front of "idea" sends a clear message: Don't suggest an idea unless it's going to be BIG.

What is happening in these situations is a very subtle form of pre-judging new thinking that blocks creativity and a vibrant flow of ideas. Nobody knows if a new idea will be big. Setting that expectation before anyone voices a new possibility restricts the number of ideas a group will even suggest. A big idea is a lot more likely to emerge from among a thousand possibilities than from a tiny trickle of ideas already pre-filtered (potentially multiple times) to only those that feel big before someone takes a risk to suggest it.

## Generating 1,000 Ideas (Maybe Even Big Ones)

Start your cross-functional team toward finding a potential big idea by stating your objective as generating 1,000 ideas of any size, shape, or form. To achieve this, follow these three steps:
1. Identify targeted opportunities
2. Imagine innovative ideas
3. Implement the best ideas with impact

## Identifying Targeted Opportunities

First, ask strong questions looking toward the future. Try this first round of future-oriented questions to get the group's take on what's important for the team or organization:

- What is our organization passionate about doing for our people and our customers? Are we doing it well?
- What are we best at and where can we continue to excel?
- Who will our customers be five years from now? What do we think will be important for us to deliver in best serving them?

- What capabilities do we want to put in place to stretch our organization and better serve our audiences?
- What are the things we need to concentrate on to dramatically exceed our goals and objectives?

Next, spend time with a set of bigger questions. Asking challenging and disruptive questions will lead to bolder thinking:

- What would our goals look like if we 10x'd all of them?
- How will we solve everything that has seemed impossible for us to do previously?
- What internal policies and procedures should we start ignoring immediately to innovate faster?
- What can we purposely break to force cutting all ties to how we do things now?
- What can we do to totally befuddle our competitors, creating chaos and inaction?
- What are the stupid unwritten rules in our industry we must upend right away?
- How can we double our innovation capacity by the end of the day tomorrow?
- What can we do to be 10x faster than we are now doing _____? (Fill in any area where you need greater speed)

This second set of questions should surface ideas people think and chatter about but never suggest at meetings because they imagine they are too difficult or painful to address.

Devote 30 minutes to each of these groups of questions, setting an expectation of finishing the hour with 150 ideas. Afterward, allow everyone 5–10 sticky notes or check marks to identify the ideas the group thinks will matter most to the organization's future success. Next, select the 20 ideas with the most interest from the team. Go back through those priorities and re-state them, if needed, so they are complete and targeted. For example, re-write a goal such as: "big improvements in computers" to "a dramatically lighter, more compact laptop computer."

With this initial forward-looking focus, the team is primed to tackle multiple questions that explore alternatives to approach the 20 important objectives.

### Imagining Innovative Ideas

For step two, divide the group into teams of three or four people. Assign the 20 objectives across the small groups. Then, have the groups spend five minutes per objective coming up with ideas related to the current question by answering:

- What are our CURRENT IDEAS for accomplishing this objective? (Target 10 ideas per objective)
- How would our strongest, smartest COMPETITOR attack this objective? (Target 10 ideas per objective)
- If no one could stop us from doing the WILDEST THINGS IMAGINABLE, how would we approach this objective? (Target 15 ideas per objective)
- If we had to accomplish this objective as SIMPLY as possible, how would we remove steps, costs, and complexity to bring it to life rapidly? (Target 10 ideas per objective)
- From all the ideas so far for this objective, what are VARIATIONS, COMBINATIONS, or ALTERNATIVES that are smart ways to accomplish it? (Target 5 ideas per objective)

When the groups finish answering each question for all the objectives they are working on, one team member takes the objectives and answers and moves to another small group for the next question. This provides continuity (someone has background on all the ideas) while giving each small group a chance to come up with ideas for as many objectives as possible.

As you move through this exercise, you may wonder what ideas are going to have the most potential. There are two informal cues to pay attention to as the ideas are flowing. Listen for these two reactions:

- A noticeable "Oooooh," usually followed by a breathless silence as the idea sinks in
- An idea is met with loud laughter

These are both early indicators of intriguing ideas. The "Oooooh" and silence signals that the group was surprised by the idea, but is already thinking about the potential. The laughter indicates an idea that pushes outside the group's comfort zone, which means it is edgy in a potentially game-changing way.

And if you are doing the math at home, when you're done, it works out to be 50 ideas (across 5 questions) for 20 different objectives. That totals 1,000 ideas! And the great thing about 1,000 ideas (as opposed to 15 ideas) is you have real possibilities for game-changers!

### Attracting Always Includes Implementing

What are you going to do after you've attracted the right people, perspectives, and imaginations to come up with 1,000 ideas?

You need to implement!

How do you move from 1,000 ideas to the ones you will act on to create dramatic results?

The prospect of trying to review and to narrow that many ideas to a manageable group you can more readily work with may seem like a daunting task. One thousand ideas don't sort *themselves* into prioritized groups and self-identify as the best ones.

In answer to your question, there's good news and *other* news when it comes to this challenge.

The good news is that you can apply a structured, strategic, and efficient approach to assessing a large number of ideas just as you just used comparable approaches to generate the ideas.

The other news is that we'll tackle that topic in Chapter 9. If you can't wait, you can head there now. If you can muster the patience, how about investing the time to understand the powers from *Connecting* and *Encouraging* in the next chapters? Then, we'll pick up on what to do with your 1,000 ideas to transform the future of your organization!

# 7

# Making Unexpected Connections

A number of years ago, I was driving across town and a billboard caught my attention. It featured a prominent and surprising phrase: Flexible perfectionists. A local company was seeking unique and versatile people to fuel its continued growth. The hiring website listed on the billboard expanded the list of diverse talents to include outgoing introverts, impulsive planners, and collaborative rebels, among others.

The billboard might as well have said, "Hiring Idea Magnets!"

Pairing diverse perspectives is fundamental to creative problem solving. Generating the most interesting new possibilities comes from a willingness and ability to simultaneously approach opportunities in more than one way. That is why Idea Magnets are such great "and" thinkers. It's all about finding ways you can have this AND that to discover new ways of thinking and doing.

Idea Magnets boost creativity by embracing perspectives people naturally see as inherently contradictory. They put people and situations together in unexpected ways to fuel creativity. They capitalize on disparate pairings others would never think to combine.

Idea Magnets also display talents often seen as opposites. For example, they are strong at both generating ideas and prioritizing them. They imagine fanciful possibilities and uncover ways to implement them to create results. Using creative formulas, Idea Magnets combine surprising possibilities to generate abundant ideas.

### A Powerfully Influential Connection

I met Chuck Dymer early in my corporate career. He was the first person I heard deliver an in-depth presentation on creative thinking skills. He captivated me with his message. We hired Chuck to facilitate multiple high-impact strategic innovation sessions at Yellow. His creativity techniques helped us generate an amazing volume of transformational ideas as we reimagined our service and marketing model.

Chuck is a quintessential Idea Magnet, and a creative mentor for me. He has done more than any other individual to school me in creative thinking processes and their importance to business success. Chuck is a true master at what he does.

At Yellow, we adopted many of Chuck's techniques into our strategic planning methodology. Our market planning team incorporated creative thinking to help internal clients generate ideas. As we designed strategy workshops, we leaned heavily on what we learned from Chuck. This was so much the case that someone once said to me, "You've changed your job into Chuck's job."

That was essentially accurate. Suffice it to say, there wouldn't be a Brainzooming if I had never met Chuck.

We hired Chuck to speak to our marketing department's quarterly meeting. At one point, Chuck pulled out a copy of that morning's *USA Today* and highlighted an article he'd read right before our meeting. You would think the article had nothing to do with anything about us, marketing, or our company. Then suddenly, he made an amazing connection, unveiling how the article was EXACTLY about our situation. He expanded our thinking through sharing a random article and making it integral to his pre-planned talk in a novel, impactful way.

That event influenced me tremendously.

I wanted my creative thinking skills to be that strong. I wanted to be able to use something random and make a valuable, intriguing connection in real time.

My reaction to Chuck's talk led to exploring methods for how to boost my creative thinking skills to fashion comparable intriguing connections.

Years later, in a strategic planning session Chuck and I co-facilitated for a client's future vision, he did it again. As he discussed a forward-looking analysis we prepared for our client, he produced the *USA Today* from that morning and connected it to what we were covering during the day.

He once again surprised me, triggering an important reminder about how Chuck's uncanny ability to find unexpected, creatively-rich connections launched me on a multi-year-path to find ways to better exploit the power of intriguing connections for generating plentiful ideas.

## All the Ways to Compare This AND That

Finding more connections between more things catalyzes creativity. Connections allow you to dramatically expand the range of possibilities you consider. More possibilities lead to more ideas from which to choose.

Making idea-stimulating connections begins with embracing "ands," especially the "ands" that link polar opposite items and situations. The tension and conflict in associating apparently ridiculous things sparks new, Idea Magnet-caliber thinking.

To demonstrate the rich opportunity in forging unusual connections, let's tackle the ultimate in difficult, "you can't make this comparison" pairings: apples and oranges.

Who knows how many innovative possibilities have been thwarted by claims that a potentially breakthrough creative combination is *like comparing apples and oranges*?

This phrase is a convenient block for unfamiliar thinking.

And it's incorrect.

There are many ways apples and oranges are comparable, especially when you think about them in a more general way. Stepping back from the specifics of a situation and seeing it less distinctly, you open numerous creative ways to compare things. The ability to effectively generalize produces tremendous creative thinking power. It's an ability that Idea Magnets continually wield to generate more ideas.

To make the point, generalizing apples and oranges provides multiple valuable comparisons. Beyond both of them being fruits, they are both sold in grocery stores, could complement each other in recipes, and are viable options for when you are hungry.

Is the point becoming clear? If the ultimate two things people say you can't compare can be matched up in multiple ways, ANY thing, situation, opportunity or challenge has ample potential for creativity-inducing pairings. The hurdle is, if you aren't a natural at identifying unusual connections how can you improve to the point that it becomes simple and routine? Fortunately, there are creative formulas you can try.

* * *

## In Action: Uncovering Compelling Connections to Generate Creativity

Many people wouldn't associate formulas with creative thinking. Yet, formulas are powerful tools to ensure your creativity is freed from depending on random or hoped-for inspiration. Creative inspiration is great, although you can't always count on it to strike when you need it most. A creative formula, on the other hand, is ready whenever you need to generate new ideas. As you develop a repertoire of successful creative formulas, you can combine and rearrange them to devise additional ways to generate ideas. And as much as you master them, you can teach them to others.

Let's explore a variety of ways to sharpen and develop your skills at uncovering the compelling connections that produce innovative thinking.

## Applying Apples and Oranges Thinking

The apples and oranges example showed that conventional wisdom about the best ways to make smart connections limits possibilities. With a little imagination (and the help of creative formulas), you can spot the fruitful connections all around. Here are seven ways you can use apples and oranges thinking to make unexpected connections:

1. How or where can you apply a comparable **PROCESS** to each one?
2. What are situations where you can **MIX** the two things?
3. Where could either one successfully **REPLACE** the other one?
4. What are the most **PREPOSTEROUS** situations in which these two things could find themselves linked?
5. How can you exploit the **MALLEABLE** characteristics of the two items to transform them into something nearly identical?
6. What **RANDOM** twists or turns would lead to new connection between the two?
7. What possibilities are there to pair the situations to something even more **UNLIKE** the two things?

Run through any of these questions in your head to imagine connections. To continue improving your connection-making skills, pick unlikely pairs of things—in your professional or personal life or even completely removed from your world—and challenge yourself to see how many innovative connections you can imagine.

**This is Like That**

"Our business is unique. It's not like other businesses."

How many times have you heard that statement, especially from executives reluctant to think creatively and strategically?

Variations on this comment have prompted me to blurt out, more than once, "Those same problems exist in lots of companies. Don't think your situation is so special."

When executives mistakenly cocoon themselves in the belief that they can't learn from anything outside their immediate competitive sets, it's good to shatter any unfounded security.

One inspiration to help business people see how their situations resemble others is based on the ancient story about the blindfolded men that each touched varied parts of an elephant. Without the ability to experience the elephant in total, each one had a very different perception of an elephant because of a limited sensory view. Flipping that approach dramatically increases the potential strategic connections. Isolating one part of a situation and ignoring everything else allows you to identify all the similar situations that match only that one element. Just as the blindfolded men all came away with different comparisons, creating your own isolated view will grow the diversity of your strategic connections.

If you can run through multiple isolated perspectives on your own, that's fantastic. If not, invite others to participate. Consider separate parts of the whole, independent of any part of the bigger situation. This is an instance where people not agreeing on what they are looking at is a benefit, not a problem.

71

To facilitate thinking about parts of your situation on your own, use this exercise to focus on narrow aspects of any opportunity, or challenge. It is based around a completing a sentence with two blanks:

*Our situation _____ like _____.*

The first blank is filled with sense (feels, looks, sounds, smells), goal (accomplishes something, serves audiences, communicates), and action (behaves, moves, turns into something) words.

What completes the second blank? The multiple answers to that blank come from the intriguing connections you imagine. With just a few rounds of this exercise, you can generate an ample list of innovation-inducing comparisons to fill the question's second blank.

On your first pass, don't worry about how closely each potential strategic connection fits your situation. What's more important is the volume of ideas, along with their specificity, boldness, and distance from your original situation. After you've generated a healthy list of actual strategic connections, refine and narrow the list to those that have the best possibilities for stimulating further strategic thinking.

## Mega Connections

Reality TV shows are outstanding sources for creative thinking formulas. I look to programs where people are learning how to do new things or that feature experts in unique creative environments. Imagining how the people on the shows come up with ideas routinely inspires new creative exercises.

*Diners, Drive-Ins, and Dives* is a favorite for robust, connection-based creativity formulas. The program visits unusual restaurants around the country that employ all sorts of intriguing modifications related to typical food. The culinary Idea Magnets the show features abundantly use *ands* to combine multiple influences and produce extreme creativity. You can boost bold connections by applying prevalent *and*-based themes from the show, such as:

- **Diversity**: How can we smash together multiple, diverse influences no one in their right mind would ever consider putting together?
- **Volume**: What are additional ingredients we could incorporate?
- **Surprise**: What ingredients could we combine that nobody would ever expect to be thrown together?
- **Repetitiveness**: What are all the ways we could use one thing in *every* way possible?
- **Adding Time**: What are ways to spend more time than anyone would ever expect to prepare something before we sell it?
- **Enlarging**: How might we exaggerate the portions so they're 5 times (or more) larger than normal?
- **Eclecticism**: In what ways can we cultivate, curate, and celebrate a total mash-up of unusual ingredients in what we produce?

The apples and oranges, this is *like* that, and mega connections formulas can produce numerous creative possibilities for your team to pursue.

# In Action: Introducing Your Team to Fruitful Connections

While you work to stretch your own abilities in making creative connections, the goal is to grow your team's capabilities. Idea Magnets teach creative formulas (such as those in the first part of the chapter) to their teams. They also shape their teams' environments and practices to leverage connection-making throughout their organizations.

### Cultivating Porous Organizations

Let's look at how one Idea Magnet encourages what he has dubbed a *porous organization*. A porous organization allows ideas to readily move in, move out, and connect to cultivate significant innovations.

I met Joe Batista in his role as the Chief Creatologist at Hewlett Packard. He had responsibility for making connections between client business needs and available HP assets (often applied in new or unconventional ways) to create breakthrough business results. The opportunity in front of Joe was large: HP applied a multi-billion-dollar annual target for realizing new value by creatively solving B2B client business challenges through Joe's innovative approach.

Joe focused on going beyond a closed innovation model to explore internal research in new ways. He pushed on the company's boundaries for opportunities to apply disconnected technologies. Instead of looking at standard descriptions and uses for applications, Joe applied an asset-oriented mindset. He generalized what a technology could do and combined organizationally-dispersed internal assets to develop solutions. Even though capabilities may have been there already, no one was bundling them to address emerging client needs. To put it succinctly, Joe's role was to connect multiple environments to the flow of ideas, resources, and assets to expand the range, pace, and impact of innovation.

Does it sound like a perfect job for an Idea Magnet?

While Joe can't share his proprietary methodologies and strategies outside the organization, you can translate his approach to your own organization. A big piece comes through pairing diverse activities and situations to create high-impact results.

### Innovative Thinking in Pairs

Pairing people with diverse perspectives is fundamental to developing Idea Magnets. Likewise, creating an environment that pairs diverse *settings and activities* provides the backdrop for Idea Magnets to flourish.

To help your team foster an ever-increasing number of connections, routinely vary the way the team works together. If they typically work in a large group, create an environment where they can work solo or in small groups. Since people tend to gravitate toward working with the same people, actively manage the work pairings. One possibility? Create unlikely pairings of people and have them find the common connections they share.

Since not everyone will be their most effective contributing in the same ways, allow individuals to work and contribute solo while taking advantage of the team's combined thinking skills at other times.

The mix of individual, small, and large group activities creates both quiet and noisy settings for creative activities. Use all these settings based on what works best for your team given the task at hand.

As you bring your team together, combine dependable creative formulas and new inspirations as potential additions to your creative tool kit. You can introduce new frameworks by customizing familiar ones for the team's current challenge.

Another variable at your disposal is the level of seriousness of the topics your team is tackling. It's tough to be serious and creative for an extended period without a fun break. At Brainzooming, we call these *mental lemon sorbets*. Giving the group permission to imagine the wackiest connections possible is a good way to lighten the mood, create laughs, and probably find the breakthrough idea you have been seeking.

When it comes to creative thinking activities to use with your team, you also want to keep things fluid with:

- Long and short activities, so you can incorporate including multiple thinking perspectives.
- Some activities that expand the number of ideas and others that let the team narrow and select high potential ideas.
- Both thinking and doing. The doing times allow for developing concepts, prototyping ideas, and creating implementation plans.

Managing all these variables provides your team a robust environment to start imagining and working with powerful creative connections.

### Opening Boundaries

How do you next get an organization to open itself to become a giant Idea Magnet?

Joe Batista talks about porous organizations. These are ones where ideas move in and out freely. That's not automatically an easy task, especially for organizations that have gained success and flourished looking at themselves, their markets, and their competitors in only one way.

76

Early in the days of smartphones, I spoke at a technology innovation conference with a C-level executive from a cellular phone company. He highlighted the incredible number of photographs being taken and sent via cell phones monthly, even in the early 2000s.

Two years later, I saw an executive from Kodak speak. The company was already getting its clock cleaned through digital photography's emergence. Nonetheless, he spent his entire talk touting the attractiveness of printing things! There was little recognition of alternative means of communicating and transmitting images and the impact on Kodak.

It would have been interesting to sit inside Kodak in the years leading up to the explosion of digital photography to understand why cell phones were never considered credible competitive threats.

The scary implication is the inability of a company to open its horizons and realize that not all great ideas and competitive threats will come from organizations that look like themselves. Cell phones don't look like cameras, and the images that they produce may fall short of those produced by the highest-quality digital cameras. Yet, for capturing and sharing images, a smartphone is *the* camera for most people.

## Opening Up to Other Companies

That's where strategic analogs are important. These are organizations that perform comparable functions to your own brand, even if they are in far-removed industries. Strategic analogs are great sources of ideas to shape your organization's innovative possibilities.

How can you productively imagine a whole variety of strategic analogies with your team? You can use the questions that follow to help your team think about companies like your own that are far removed competitively. Step one is to describe your own organization in terms that are as general as possible.

Then, working from the general description, use this list of questions to expand the range and depth of potential strategic analogies:

- What companies have similar sizes and organizational structures to ours?
- Who are our strategic partners?
- Who are our primary competitors?
- What companies provide substitutes for what we offer to customers?
- What other companies serve the same customers?
- What other companies have similar strategies?
- What industries have similar operations or sales structures?
- What companies have similar cost structures?
- What companies employ similar processes to the ones we use?
- What companies are trying to innovate in similar ways?
- What companies of our size have similar ownership and/or financial structures?
- What companies that do the same general things we do have comparable business situations?
- What other companies that share our general business category are most like us?
- What other companies are facing comparable competitive dynamics?
- What other companies are facing comparable cost pressures?
- What industries and companies look or behave like ours? Why/how?

Answering these questions will provide a huge head start in seeing potential competitors, partners, and idea sources among comparable organizations that look nothing like your own today.

### What's It Like?

When you fully exploit connections, you can easily generate innovative ideas for your organization from the vantage point of another, perhaps wildly different company. Using a robust perspective from which to innovate creates dramatic results. An exercise called *What's It Like?* is a convenient way to combine all the aspects you need for your team to perform as nimble Idea Magnets, even if that's been a struggle previously.

I was speaking to someone who worked at a hospital. She bemoaned a recent strategy planning session at her facility. She said it was clear the doctors didn't want to be there, the staff was bored, and it ended with no new future-looking ideas surfacing.

I suggested how *What's It Like?* could have completely changed the dynamics of the hospital's exploration. First, I asked her to describe the hospital's situation. We generalized five characteristics to describe the hospital's focus as:

- Fixing things
- Taking care of customers
- Employing people
- Providing opportunities for learning
- Making money

Reviewing the list to identify a comparable organization from whose perspective to innovate, we decided all five characteristics matched The Home Depot.

Working with the perspective of The Home Depot, we started Brainzooming what The Home Depot would do if it were running the hospital. Ideas began flowing, including the idea of the hospital offering do-it-yourself surgery. While she scoffed at the idea, I pointed out people decades earlier would have said no patient would ever perform medical tests. Now, however, many personal medical tests line the shelves at drugstores. I can see some version of do-it-yourself surgery (assisted with robotics) becoming common within twenty years, even though it was so future-looking as to be laughable several years ago.

My point to her was that if the hospital truly wanted to place some big bets on future innovations, *What's It Like?* had already yielded one strong candidate in only a few minutes.

*What's It Like?* is simple to use:

1. Pick your business opportunity or challenge.
2. List a variety of its characteristics, potentially generalizing the characteristics even further.
3. Select an organization facing a comparable situation.
4. Imagine how the other organization, given its different view of your situation, would approach your initiative.

With *What's It Like?,* you get away from the concept of industry best practices. As an Idea Magnet, your goal is thinking of dramatically innovative ideas for your organization no one in your industry is practicing!

\* \* \*

Why so many tools and questions for creating connections? Because they are so important to Idea Magnets performing strongly and developing the same capabilities in those around them. With robust tools and lots of encouragement, Idea Magnet-level innovation is within anyone's grasp.

Speaking of encouragement from Idea Magnets, after working with Chuck Dymer on multiple projects, he said something that changed my life: "You make other people more creative just by cheering them on." While always enjoying participating in brainstorming sessions, the impact of personally encouraging others had never occurred to me.

Chuck's comment caused me to more deliberately cultivate this talent and use it more widely. This ultimately led to Brainzooming and writing *Idea Magnets*.

In the next chapter, let's look more closely at how encouragement is integral to spreading a passion for becoming an Idea Magnet among everyone you know.

# 8

# Encouraging People and Ideas

Idea Magnets are dynamic cheerleaders. They understand creatively fruitful ways that people, behaviors, and experiences support and challenge others to generate tremendous positive impacts. Idea Magnets encourage those around them through both boldness and subtlety, and, even when they are not even personally present.

## Encouraging with All the Right Words

Laura Schmidt is the founder of notes to self® socks. These socks feature words of encouragement and aspiration on the toes and soles in an array of colors. The socks remind you that, "I am brave," "I am a great friend," "I am amazing," and a variety of other inspiration-boosting messages. While you may not *see* the encouraging words with your shoes on, every time you put them on you experience the encouragement, and begin associating the sentiment with the colors of the words and socks. No matter what you're doing, glancing at your feet recalls the special note of encouragement you chose that day.

I met Laura while delivering a workshop on social media for business. The presentation included a video I shot in my neighborhood about the creative lesson in finding treasure in someone else's trash.

Laura recognized the neighborhood in the video and approached me afterward to chat. We quickly discovered that we lived barely a mile away from each other. She told me all about notes to self® socks and her mission to spread words of encouragement through footwear. She also promised to send me a pair of orange, "I am brave" socks to add to my orange sock collection.

Several years later, returning home, I found a bag on the door handle of our house. A phone message from Laura explained that her newest notes to self® design (which were in the bag) were orange and imprinted with, "I am creative." Because of wearing orange socks daily and all the Brainzooming content on creativity, I had inspired Laura to design them.

The orange "I am creative" sock story (and giving pairs away to attendees) quickly became a highlight of keynote presentations and workshops I deliver!

Laura Schmidt brought together people (me, and ultimately everyone in the groups I speak to), behaviors (me wearing orange socks daily), and experience (providing ongoing encouragement) as inspiration to introduce just one of the more than 60 notes to self® socks. And Laura has already spread her inspirational message via the TODAY Show and Good Morning America.

## Encouraging Unseen Talents

Individuals often struggle to recognize their own talents, especially non-traditional ones that could bring value to the workplace. Idea Magnets typically have deep insights into team members' seemingly hidden potential strengths. In these situations, they step in (and sometimes step away) to draw out Idea Magnet-level talents.

I experienced this phenomenon personally. One of my Idea Magnets forced me to use a talent I'd never considered beneficial in a work setting. We were holding our first national sales meeting at Yellow. Greg Reid, as the CMO, was emceeing the meeting where baseball legend Tommy Lasorda was the keynote speaker. The night before the meeting, Greg told me he needed to spend time with Tommy the next afternoon. As a result, he wanted me to emcee the 600-person meeting. And oh, by the way, there was no script; just a group of rather dry senior management speakers to introduce.

The next day, I had to get up in front of the group and be funny, motivate them, and even try to get senior leaders off the stage. By the end of the afternoon, I went from the entire sales team and operation management group seeing me as a quiet research guy to experiencing me as a funny, completely at-ease emcee. Greg saw those possibilities in me, even though I missed seeing them. By backing away, he pushed me on the path to being a more visible creative leader. In one afternoon, Greg's insight into my skills and his willingness to surrender the spotlight reshaped the rest of my career.

The opportunity for those types of impacts prompts Idea Magnets to continually look for opportunities to place team members in roles that bring out hidden talents they might not otherwise display and develop.

## Experiences Big and Small

Idea Magnets encourage creativity by facilitating unique creative experiences.

This idea came home for me when we designed and facilitated a 200-person Brainzooming workshop on increasing the availability of digital tools for all community segments in the Kansas City metropolitan area, where I live. Bringing together this community group was unique in that these exact participants would never collaborate again. This was the *only* day they would ever experience exciting, creative thinking with these individuals as a team.

We provided questions that each small group used to identify its members' aspirations and ideas. Across all the independent responses, the small groups aligned around nine themes to shape the community's digital inclusion strategy. The day's work with this unique group led to identifying multiple insights and constituent groups that the initiative's formal leaders had overlooked.

Reflecting on the event later, it struck me how unique experiences can encourage new thinking and ideas. While that sometimes happens on a large scale, as in the community event, it can also take place on a small scale, with even just a few team members working together. You can manage the mix of people, behaviors, and experiences to realize creative objectives:

- **People:** Involve special guest speakers, experts, and consultants
- **Behaviors:** Creative exercises, team recreational activities, making varied things (presentations, videos, etc.), extending gratitude

85

- **Experiences:** Offsite meetings at zoos, field locations, and hotel conference settings; fun, challenging and frustrating projects.

These are all great ways to break through the routine of the same people looking at each other daily as creativity stagnates. No matter the specific situation, Idea Magnets use all kinds of experiments to encourage their own creativity and that of their teams.

* * *

# In Action: Encouraging Yourself First

It doesn't matter how high up you are on the organizational ladder, everyone needs encouragement. Finding it, especially at a senior level, can present a challenge. It's vital, especially for Idea Magnets, to be adept at encouraging themselves if they are going to effectively encourage others. That starts with knowing who to reach out to for support throughout your career.

### Idea Magnets for Idea Magnets

Idea Magnets need their own strategic mentors. If you are fortunate, you will enjoy multiple strategic mentors throughout your life who are best suited to your present career stage. Your current strategic mentors should be your first stop when you need an encouraging word or suggestion.

Ideally, you've stayed close to previous mentors who knew you during earlier career phases. Even if someone isn't a primary strategic mentor in your career now, relive the old days. Your mentor may remember details, challenges, and successes you've forgotten but would do well to remember. Share how you are applying things you learned from your mentor. That's returning value in exchange for the value you received.

Reach out to others who inspire you – whether you know them personally or only from afar. One way to keep track of everyone that fits into one of these two categories is by creating a "top 100" list of people who personally define you. A special edition of *People Magazine* inspired the idea for creating this list. While the *People Magazine* list was filled with popular celebrities the magazine had shaped our culture, yours will focus on identifying personal inspirations that have shaped you.

Creating your list prompts a healthy dose of personal reflection. It also makes you consider whether you've sufficiently recognized, thanked, and passed along what you've learned from your top 100 personal influencers.

Your list doesn't have to be in any specific order. The objective is simply to identify everyone first and evaluate your list later. Creating my own list proved tremendously worthwhile. Since writing the initial version, I have gone back through it, replacing some people with new ones not included in the first draft.

With a relatively short time investment, a top 100 list provides substantial insight into your life's greatest influencers. Review the list of individuals currently playing a role in your life as well as others that you have not spoken with lately. They could be a source of encouragement. For those you don't personally know, revisit works of theirs that originally influenced you. Adjust the list over time to include new influencers that reliably encourage you at that life stage.

## Giving and Receiving Encouragement

Idea Magnets mentor and share their life and creative strategies to influence others. Finding the right mix between teaching and giving your team room to grow on its own is vital.

Balance sharing your knowledge and inclinations with team members' needs so they have room to develop their own styles. Idea Magnets in training can only build distinctive styles if you remain open and refrain from over-instructing them.

If things don't go as planned when you are providing more space to team members, don't rush to identify the specific problem. Try simply letting them know there is an opportunity to improve the quality or creativity of what the team is trying to accomplish. Invite team members to ponder the issue, address what they discover, and then share suggestions. This puts team members in charge of identifying, determining, and making the appropriate responses to any performance shortfalls.

Provide ample room for team members to disagree and interpret your input. Allow team members to self-diagnose and express their own, perhaps contrary, perspectives to yours. Team members may have on-target creative perspectives beyond what the Idea Magnet imagines or readily understands.

Idea Magnets realize that encouraging others is impossible if they dictate exactly what they expect and want. You need to give experienced team members latitude to chart their strategies to achieve shared objectives.

Just as you need to give team members creative room and encouragement to develop ideas, you need to open space for them to share their ideas and strategic suggestions with you. Provide that space by displaying behaviors that make it clear you're not going to manage every detail and want to learn and develop with their help. Some examples:

- Pinpoint your weaknesses and identify team members whose strengths can compensate.
- State project objectives without dictating *how* they should be accomplished.
- Hit your deadlines so you don't delay others.
- Provide background on how you make decisions and judge performance so they can act without constantly checking with you.
- Allow people who have demonstrated appropriate responsibility and ownership to lead more.
- Listen to ideas from others, responding quickly and clearly when your team seeks input.
- Share your input when it's needed and there is still time to act, but then hold your peace.
- Stick with the decisions you make so others can confidently act on them.

These behaviors lead those you work with to use their talents and meaningfully contribute instead of order-taking and risking second-guessing.

### Following Conversations

One day on his show, radio call-in host Dr. Ray Guarendi discussed following conversations. As "Dr. Ray" describes it, "following a conversation" involves actively listening to another person, instead of biding your time until you can talk more about yourself.

Getting better at following a conversation involves:

- Asking a next question that allows the other person to keep talking
- Making an on-topic comment directed at the other person's perspective and not your own
- Giving the other person space (i.e., nods of encouragement) to keep talking
- Not expending mental energy thinking about what you'll say next
- Elaborating on something the other person said that builds on what the person is talking about
- Turning the conversation toward the other person and away from yourself

Using these techniques, you follow the other person through the points he or she is making instead of cutting them short and taking over the conversation.

### Gratitude

Idea Magnets readily express sincere gratitude.

One long-standing answer for how to best express gratitude comes via Dale Carnegie. He offered a robust prescription for gratitude in "How to Win Friends and Influence People" in the 1930s: Be "hearty in your approbation and lavish in your praise." To expand on putting Carnegie's advice into action, sincere gratitude requires confidence that another person's work does not threaten your own work.

When Idea Magnets embrace lavishly praising others, they realize displaying gratitude does not show up as a line item in any organization's income and expense statement. Even when the ability to show appreciation with extrinsic motivators (i.e., salary increases, bonuses, bigger titles) is limited, nobody in

Finance is checking to see if you exceeded your "thank you" budget!

* * *

# In Action: Encouraging Team Creativity

We've all seen average performers in business rise to greater accomplishments when others cheer them on and encourage their success. That's why Idea Magnets act as *business fans* for their team members. A business fan establishes solid connections with team members, genuinely finding things about them to celebrate, emulate, and encourage in the rest of the team. It means creating an environment where the team knows an Idea Magnet looks at them and thinks "we," not "them." And when solid team members are legitimately struggling to perform, a business fan sticks with them and encourages their efforts to get back on track.

For all the fanfare about celebrating failures, an innovative workplace culture recognizes and celebrates trying and learning, progress and determination, AND success.

Leaders protect new, challenging, and unusual ideas. What are you doing to protect those ideas in your organization?

* * *

### Creating a Diverse Team

You might think an Idea Magnet would want to surround him or herself with only the top creative talent. Instead, they realize that multiple thinking orientations working together produce the best innovative thinking—

far better than with a group composed entirely of classically creative types.

The similarity in thinking styles and perspectives among people who view themselves as creative lacks diversity. The group may feel it's creative, but risks missing important links to what will move an organization forward. That's why you want to include experts throughout an organization solving challenges creatively.

### Tapping New Team Members' Ideas

Attracting new creative leaders is routine for Idea Magnets. The question is how to take the best advantage of these fresh perspectives when new members are integrating into the team.

Sometimes, as the team leader, you may want to keep a new team member more focused on the team's future than its history. This helps maintain perspective in situations where you need completely new ideas or reactions.

Typically, though, you want to give someone new the appropriate background to allow them to perform better, function faster and avoid re-learning lessons the "organization" already knows. As you share this information, don't constrain a new person with repeated comparisons to how things have been done. The old team formation has changed—reset your expectations and aspirations accordingly.

Since you've brought someone onto the team for new ideas and expertise, encourage the person to share and try new ideas. Be a cheerleader and enabler for making new ideas into reality. Improve your team's daily performance by being the biggest fan of all team members, by actively rooting for their individual and collective successes.

## Developing New Idea Magnets

Idea Magnets develop other Idea Magnets through enthusiastically encouraging team members' individual and collective strengths and performance.

One way that happens is through clearly sharing bold aspirations to engage, align, and motivate the team. Vagueness under the guise of creative freedom can lead to significant wasted time. This happens when team members must guess what a leader wants and simply hope to get close. Idea Magnets empower their teams by sharing objectives *and* providing latitude for team members to develop unforeseen or unexpected ideas.

You can create openings for personal ownership through sharing criteria or guidelines that team members can use to make independent decisions. You can also have team members take on shadow roles, such as working with an Idea Magnet on every step of a big initiative, before assuming greater responsibility.

## Showcasing Diverse Talents and Perspectives

Confident leaders realize they are smarter and more creative themselves when surrounded by other smart, creative individuals. That's why an Idea Magnet showcases the talents of team members in every possible situation. Developing Idea Magnets within the team attracts others seeking comparable opportunities for greater career growth and recognition.

Strong leaders also make it safe and easy for team members to challenge their ideas with beneficial, even contrary perspectives.

This happens through:

- Seeking input from junior team members initially and senior team members later. This allows less-tenured individuals to comment without undue influence from senior people.
- Asking open-ended questions that don't presuppose preferred answers. This allows room for others to respond without tipping your hand on any pre-existing opinions.
- Responding to challenges with additional questions and listening instead of mounting an immediate defense of your own ideas.
- Setting an expectation that team members offer potential solutions when calling attention to unresolved issues.

## Encouraging without Crushing Ideas

Within the team environment, it is possible for a leader to over-celebrate new ideas in a way that crushes creativity. Sound preposterous? Here's an example.

Suppose the team is doing the creative thinking to generate new ideas for a project, both alone and in small groups. When ideas are works in progress, supportive comments from the boss are helpful to further creativity and additional thinking. If an ultra-positive leader shares only effusive praise for an idea under development that is new to the entire group, it is challenging for someone else to say, "That idea could be stronger strategically," or "There are other possibilities to consider." A team member can offer these perspectives, but it is awkward when the leader's praise makes a weak idea seem to be the best creative breakthrough ever. Others may see trying to adapt or challenge the idea as sabotaging another's creativity.

A better leadership approach is to introduce a new idea, credit the originator, and remark positively on its possibilities and potential to grow and develop. After sharing the idea's status (i.e., it's open for consideration all the way up to its being a done deal), the leader can invite team members to comment, build on, and adapt it.

This strategy balances being positive and leaving room for other team members to provide their unencumbered creative thinking.

## An Encouraging Response for Every Idea

In my corporate days, I was assigned to work with competitive companies our corporation had recently purchased. The objective was to help them become better strategic thinkers and marketers. One ground rule? I had to refrain from telling them *what* to do. Since all the companies competed with one another, each needed to determine its own business strategies.

When I tell people this story, they chuckle. It seems ridiculous to help a company become better at strategy and marketing without being allowed to give them direct suggestions. While this constraint may seem ridiculous, it played a fundamental role in shaping the Brainzooming method.

In designing how we would help these companies, I realized there were three possibilities whenever we asked people to generate ideas during strategic thinking exercises:

1. The answer could show their strategic thinking was in the right direction.
2. The answer could suggest their strategic thinking wasn't effective in this situation.
3. The answer could be an unanticipated surprise.

With on-target ideas (#1), it is easy to cheer them and encourage more of the same. With off-target ideas (#2), we would say, "That's great," or something similar and suggest alternatives to re-orient them toward a smarter direction. For complete surprises (#3), we used our response to either #1 or #2, depending on whether the idea was on- or off-target.

This suggests that when a team is collaborating, you don't necessarily need to respond by saying ideas or concepts are good or bad. You can, however, vary your reaction based on whether you *perceive* an idea to be good or bad. And if an idea is off-target, simply employ other creative thinking exercises to gently bring the ideas back to something smarter and more productive.

And even if the ideas offered aren't going to address the objective's immediate needs, look for ways to give them some visibility as the team's effort progresses. Try to use some aspect of them so the originator experiences a sense of contributing to the team's progress.

### Sharing an Innovation Vocabulary

A strong creative team needs a vocabulary to express bold aspirations and an innovative vision. This is particularly true when it is imperative to dramatically disrupt the status quo and launch new initiatives. If a team lacks the language and experience for bold innovation, it will likely falter. An Idea Magnet must ensure his or her organization has a sufficiently big innovation vocabulary to describe the degree of change needed to realize a bold future. This can come from actively managing the language the team uses. We've also seen success through exercises where the team works from bold words and images specifically selected to allow it to express a dramatic future vision.

## Creating High-Performing Team Members

One way you can involve a larger number of people in business creativity is by tailoring roles that match everyone's capabilities. With the right structure and support, you can uncover ways for everyone to succeed.

When a team member is struggling to fit a traditional role, look for ways to create a non-traditional role that maximizes the individual's talents. This will allow him or her to perform with greater impact than anyone might otherwise imagine.

This involves strategic and creative thinking and planning to identify how to successfully feature an unexpected person to productively contribute.

Having done this on many occasions, the person you are helping generally realizes what is happening, tries hard to make it work, and rewards your efforts with a greater appreciation and loyalty than if you'd have let them off the hook by not participating.

This idea of team members encouraging stronger performance extends to daily activities. Teams and organizations flourish when everyone works together seamlessly. It's easy, though, for individuals to focus on doing their own jobs, ignoring how their roles fit within the bigger picture. Broadening this perspective both helps the team and fosters richer connections.

Preparing to participate in a three-person Bible reading at church, our workbook suggested rehearsing all three parts aloud. My typical strategy would be to only practice what I was responsible for reading.

After rehearsing the entire piece several times, the advantage of this holistic strategy became clear. Reviewing the entire Bible reading made me very aware of the emotion and point of view of the next person I was leading up to, as well as of the person speaking right before me. It allowed me to vary my tone and be a better connector within our three-person team.

An entire team's success can improve if everyone is embracing a comparable holistic process. Anticipate what you'll be receiving from the person prior to you. What point of view, style, and expertise will this person bring to the work product for which you are assuming responsibility?

Also, consider the person to whom you'll hand off your efforts. What will they be expecting from you? How can you anticipate what they may struggle with to help them complete challenging parts more successfully?

In an Idea Magnet's team, everyone's role is to be a strong connector, planning for what comes before and after to boost the team's success.

### It's All about the Reflections

Tara Baukus Mello is the Idea Magnet behind this book. Her prayer and creative tenacity provided the inspiration into turning a presentation on Idea Magnets into the structure and content for this book. One day, during her role as the book's consulting editor, Tara called me out on one of those Facebook challenges. The deal was to share seven black and white photos across seven days with no explanations. Since we were putting Idea Magnets together, and I was still finding my way with the content, I picked the seven Idea Magnet characteristics for the photos to help the bigger messages come into focus.

I was speaking at a conference in Las Vegas when it was time for the Encourage picture. I snapped a picture of a neon *Open* sign that was attached to a bigger sign for a bar in front of the Fashion Show Mall on The Strip. The sign seemed like a perfect meme for this chapter: An Idea Magnet must be *open* to all kinds of ideas to encourage the team.

I didn't pay much attention in the moment, but the sign was surrounded by a protective Plexiglas wall. After looking at the photo, I realized the bigger message lurking in the Plexiglas: The Open sign was reflected four times in different directions within the Plexiglas.

It's one thing to encourage. Your encouragement's real impact is when it's reflected by others on the team. That's when it grows in power and impact.

The same is true with all the strategies to this point: they gain real power when they're reflected through deciding and implementing something. Let's go there next.

# 9

# Implementing for Impact

Brainstorming workshops start with the admonition not to censor ideas. Facilitators also reassure everyone that there is no such thing as a bad idea. As you move closer to deciding your strategy and how to implement it, that changes. The further you progress toward implementation, the clearer it is that some ideas are better than others.

The transition from *everything is a great idea* to *this is the only idea that makes sense for us* is a critical juncture. That's why Idea Magnets view strategic and creative options as a body of water. A pool or lake is fun to splash around in, enjoying the plentiful water and the recreation options—if you know what you're doing. If you aren't knowledgeable about your surroundings and can't negotiate the conditions, the results can be tragic.

Similarly, having plentiful ideas provides tremendous room for big strategic gains, only if you know how to select the best options and successfully implement them. If not, the results can also turn tragic.

Realizing this, Idea Magnets emphasize implementing ideas via making strategic decisions and buckling down to do the work.

### An Overlooked Idea Magnet

Before reaching this point in the writing, I'd never thought about my father, Bernie Brown, as an Idea Magnet. Sure, he had a successful career as a television and radio broadcaster in small western Kansas markets. He never left Hays, Kansas to see how he could create and realize a vision in a bigger arena, though. His entrepreneurial ventures outside broadcasting also weren't nearly as prosperous as his chosen profession.

Thinking about this chapter's topic, essentially deciding on which ideas to pursue and acting on them, made me realize my dad *did* continually apply Idea Magnet strategies.

While my dad was humble, he was proud that his salary for decades while managing the television station never exceeded $600 a month. Yes, you read that right. His salary was less than $7,000 annually as general manager of the TV station, yet he made great money. The rest of his income was a percentage of the station's monthly profits. Each month he put our family's entire livelihood on the line. To be successful, he had to guide it all: devise and implement a strong strategy, attract and cultivate a talented team, grow advertising revenues in innovative ways, and aggressively manage costs to deliver year-over-year profit increases. While I always thought about my father as being risk-averse, I realize now he constantly took on tremendous personal risk: he had to be innovative and improve business results with no personal room for failure. THAT is risky.

I knew he inspired many people. Even though he never put himself on a regional or national stage, he helped launch the careers of multiple young broadcasters who achieved notoriety in bigger venues. His recognition level in our relatively small community was widespread. It was a major reason I moved from Hays. I would always only be Bernie Brown's son, I was sure. My sense of Dad's Idea Magnet-level impact on people grew after he passed away. Many of his former employees remarked about the profound impacts he had on their lives.

Among the many lessons my father demonstrated, one pivotal one integrated both deciding and doing. It continues to provide tremendous value throughout my work life: To prioritize the volume and focus of your activities, you need to understand that much of business and life is a numbers game.

Early on, as my dad was making the transition from cutting hair in my grandfather's barber shop to broadcasting, he sold life insurance part-time. While selling insurance, he learned the critical lesson of 10:3:1. You had to make 10 calls to secure three appointments to close one sale.

If someone was willing to apply him or herself, work the equation, and stay motivated amid a 90 percent failure rate, they'd achieve success. If they applied learnings and new techniques to improve the close ratio, they could experience dramatic success. Get discouraged or shortcut the process by making too few calls, and they'd wash out.

While the ratios may differ, the principle applies to so many facets of business and life. You will notice the ratio is close to the percentages to move from ideas to workable strategies we covered in Chapter 6. Thinking about the numbers and math behind a situation is an important component of efficiently and effectively navigating through deciding and doing.

To this point, we have featured two In Action sections in each chapter. One is focused on the Idea Magnet's personal development and tools. The other translates the strategy to the Idea Magnet's team. As we address Implementing Ideas, we have structured the sections differently. Since ultimately some*one* must own responsibility for decision making, the first In Action section in this chapter focuses on strategies to make personal decision-making smart and efficient. The team-oriented In Action addresses moving from decisions to team implementation.

* * *

## In Action: Deciding

We all move through life-making, personal decisions. From what we select to wear when we get ready daily, to the foods we decide to eat, to the people we opt to spend time with, an individual has responsibility for making many decisions. Some decisions are more challenging and carry more weight than others. Usually, we can easily differentiate between important, complicated decisions and those where we must simply decide and move on.

When it comes to business decisions, we often get mired in the decision-making process. It might be because too many people (or opinions) are involved. The stakes may feel greater because the decisions could affect careers and livelihoods. In short, we bog down because business decisions can seem to carry much more weight and complexity than they actually do.

### Deciding Early About Deciding

The worst time to decide on how to decide things is when you are ready to decide things. When it is time for a decision, new issues emerge. People have already developed vested interests in certain outcomes. They are primed to call out or ignore data gaps to lean toward a particular point of view.

Well before you need to decide, identify who the decision-maker is and what information will go into the process. Identify who the decision will impact, both positively and negatively. List the expected decision-making criteria along with what specific factors will signal making one decision over another. Addressing these issues early makes decision making more simple, clear, and streamlined. That leads to effectively fast forwarding from deciding to doing!

### Interpreting Themes to Structure Decisions

One factor that slows decision-making is having so many ideas that it seems impossible to process them and move forward. With an Idea Magnet in the mix, seeming to have too many ideas is common. In these cases, identifying strategic themes is vital to efficiently framing decisions. Finding the right number and range of themes helps you balance broad strategic and creative thinking with the ability to form clear implementation steps. You can find strategic themes by looking for ideas that relate to your strategy, from natural groupings, things that happen around one another, possess similar characteristics, or are connected in some other way. The time you invest in identifying clear themes will turn into time savings during decision making.

## How Many Strategic Paths Do You Have?

As you assess strategic themes and opportunities, you may find you have only one path available to pursue a creative solution. In these cases, your focus is on how to best exploit every opportunity that one path presents. At other times, you may suspect there is only one good strategically-smart path, even though it seems as if there are multiple paths you could try. Here, you want to apply creativity to most effectively and efficiently decide which path really is the optimum one to choose.

If you face a scenario with several paths that could work with varying levels of success, the biggest creative challenge may be figuring out alternatives and contingencies to maximize results.

You could also be looking at a situation where there are lots of paths that could lead to strategic success. This is the time to narrow choices, get started, and apply your Idea Magnet skills to creatively implement and deliver amazing results.

Since you'll continually face situations with different dynamics and variables leading to success, work on honing your skills in determining how many strategic paths an opportunity offers. This helps you identify your most effective deciding *and* doing strategies.

## Quick Decisions

One way to assign the appropriate importance and time investment to decisions is by operating with some defined ground rules for making quick decisions. Using such a list can reduce needless time debating topics that don't require or justify it.

Areas that warrant quick decisions include:

- Non-strategic issues that won't matter much (such as process changes customers won't experience)
- Previous successful decisions where you already have a history for predicting the outcome
- Decisions you can easily recover from if they are poorly made
- Multiple acceptable decision options
- Opportunities related to areas you'll never be able to realistically pursue
- Situations where the time involved in considering the decision costs more in payroll hours than the decision's outcome

In all these and comparable situations, choose something quickly and move on.

### Simplifying Complex Choices

Making decisions boils down to saying *yes* or *no* to an idea, situation, or activity. When you and the team may have identified a plethora of interrelated ideas, situations, or activities, the decision, in that case, involves saying yes or no across a series of questions.

With that in mind, you must ask yourself, "What am I saying 'yes' and 'no' to?" You want to make sure that your answer is deliberate and strategic, instead of weighted toward instinct, feelings, boredom, or something else.

Being less deliberate and logical about saying "yes" or "no" isn't wrong. Making it a habit in a team setting, however, increases the challenge of learning from and to building on past successes and failures to move forward in smart, strategic ways.

Keep in mind that saying *yes* or *no* isn't a right or a wrong answer. It is simply a strategic choice framework to save time and improve the sense of direction.

You can even apply the yes-no approach when you have many different aspects to consider regarding a decision. For example, I was working with a team member struggling to create a presentation for a senior executive. She wanted to tell him so many things she believed he needed to know. There was no way he'd have the patience to hear more than three of the points she sought to make.

We used a forced comparison technique to help narrow the list of key messages. This adaptation of yes-no starts with writing all the potential options on individual sticky notes, placing them on a wall or desk. You then select two options and compare them, asking, "If I could say *yes* to only one of these options, which one would I select?" Place the option you pick at the top of the wall or desk, with the other below it. Repeat the process, picking up another sticky note, asking the same question relative to the top-most sticky note. If you select the new sticky note, it goes on top, and the others move down. If you don't select it, keep moving down and asking the selection question relative to each sticky note until it's appropriately placed.

When you've completed this decision-making technique, you should have a quick prioritization. This frees a challenged decision maker from the trap of wanting to prioritize *everything*. The technique works well either individually or with a group that's trying to prioritize choices in a variety of situations. Once you master it on your own, you can teach it to your team for when one of them owns the decision-making role.

## Life-Changing Deciding and Doing

One time, over the course of 36 hours, I faced a major decision: leave corporate life and make The Brainzooming Group a full-time business or hang on to a VP-level position at our struggling corporation. It wasn't an easy decision since its impact extended beyond me to my wife and work team. It wasn't the first time I'd been presented with a quick career choice where, within a very short time window (once it was 30 minutes), it was imperative to decide what I'd do next. At least this time, I had the opportunity to come home and talk with Cyndi and pray about whether we were ready to make a big, risky step back into the entrepreneurial world.

When faced with this major decision, I used an evaluation sheet to turn a life-changing decision into a series of yes-no questions. As the sole breadwinner for our family, I couldn't afford to make a wrong decision. Rather than trying to think through everything in my head at once and talk it out with my wife, I broke the decision into every factor I could imagine that would shape the decision—both personally and career-related. I looked at the decision across three possible scenarios: staying; leaving with a severance; or leaving without a severance. Within this structure, I deconstructed the complex decision into a bunch of straight-forward ones, revolving around whether each factor would be better within a specific scenario. I permitted the occasional question mark when I wasn't sure.

None of the decision factors had weightings. There was no attempt to use a rating scale. For me, simplicity and a quick decision were most important.

Using this simple strategic approach revealed something I never expected: walking out the door without a severance was an overwhelmingly more attractive option than staying. The format's clarity allowed for a quick double check of that surprise. With this breakdown, it was easy to see how leaving corporate life was the right choice, no matter the circumstances.

Distilling complex issues with an eye toward simplifying them can minimize being overwhelmed, drive quicker decisions, and move your team into action faster.

\* \* \*

# In Action: Idea Magnets ARE in action!

How does an Idea Magnet most effectively shift from creative thinking to deciding and then into doing?

Your organizational and market environment will impact the answers to this question. Working in a B2B marketing environment, we had to develop a knack for applying creativity quickly and directly to solve problems and act on opportunities. Our environment demonstrated little tolerance for fun, creative exploration that didn't expeditiously deliver real-world answers and impact.

In response, we removed guesswork about how to implement by developing as many checklists and standard routines as we could. This increased our velocity in moving from ideas to action.

### Helping Your Team Implement Strategy

To help their teams implement more effectively, Idea Magnets assess the best options and address implementation gaps before convening the team to launch a new initiative. This window presents an important opportunity to determine whether the strategy is ready for the team and vice versa.

Here's a checklist to take advantage of this review point. These are personal questions to assess how well

109

the chosen strategy and direction are suited to the implementation team responsible for moving forward:

- Do I personally believe in the strategy?
- Is it believable to others?
- Can I see the plan developing in a realistic way?
- Is the strategy specific and simple so team members will understand their roles and be ready to act?
- Is there support for the strategy in the places where it needs support?
- Does the team have an opportunity to weigh in and make smart adjustments to sharpen implementation?
- Are there contingencies in place to rectify potential issues?
- Are there early indicators to signal if something is amiss before it becomes critical?

Asking these questions upfront provides a head start to tackle potential implementation issues. Many *yes* answers suggest a larger number of implementation team members are well-prepared for the strongest possible performance.

Address any *no* answers you can before engaging the team to begin their implementation roles.

### Developing a Bias for Action

When shifting into implementation, the following questions can help your team translate ideas into clear, actionable tactics. This checklist helps identify potential implementation gaps, addressing the plan's clarity and specificity so the team can act.

- What will it take to accomplish this idea or objective?

- What are the first actions it will take to move forward?
- What individual will have responsibility for leading implementation overall and for each activity?
- Is it clear what we would walk out of here and do based on the tactics that are stated?

Getting this right at the start reduces the likelihood that later questions will slow or even stop implementation progress.

### Contingencies When Things Aren't Working

What does an Idea Magnet do when implementation isn't working as planned? Panicking or shutting down and not trying something different aren't options. You must be ready to try alternative strategies, because, hey, you're an Idea Magnet!

If things take a negative turn, try this checklist to quickly explore potential implementation changes:

- Is there something that *is* working that we can exploit more beneficially?
- Can we take something else we had planned and use a piece of it to fit the new expectation?
- Can we jump ahead to something that is already planned for later?
- Is it possible to scrap everything planned and start over quickly?
- If we go with a different plan, how can we contribute further progress toward our objective?
- Does someone else have a better idea than we do for how to move forward?
- How can we convince others to adopt our new ideas and regain momentum?

With planning, solid strategies to adapt, and an appreciation for flexibility, unexpected events become opportunities to reenergize and deliver results.

## Sharpening Implementation as Time Runs Down

Idea Magnets strengthen their impact by launching significant, breakthrough ideas. That is why hitting deadlines and delivering on commitments are important to Idea Magnets.

As deadlines approach, sometimes it makes sense to alter the implementation strategy to maximize the impact the team will deliver. If there is a sense that timing is in jeopardy, you can look at and manage multiple variables, including:

- **Outcomes:** Focusing on only the most important aspects, eliminating nice-to-haves and prioritizing *done* over *perfect*.
- **Decisions:** Going with high-probability answers and making time-constrained decisions.
- **Timing and Resources:** Prioritizing progress on long lead-time items, aggressively managing the to-do list, and reaching out for other resources.
- **Managing Expectations:** If the deadline and/or deliverables are in danger of being off, contact clients to better understand their critical needs and update expectations.

There's no reason to step back and wait passively to see how initiatives and projects will come to fruition. Idea Magnets are as aggressive, at managing implementation success, as they are at attracting incredible ideas.

## About Those 1,000 Ideas You Have

Remember in Chapter 6 where you developed 1,000 innovative ideas? We promised to help narrow them to a manageable subset of high-potential opportunities. Here's one way to start mining to highlight the big ideas among the 1,000 your team imagined.

### Setting the Stage

Before you narrow ideas, decide on how you'll approach the initial assessment. If you don't have a method you already use to prioritize ideas, consider separating the ideas by the time or ease to bring them to life. Then compare each to how dramatically different it is from to what's out there today.  Here's how you can depict these dimensions:

|  | A Variation on Current Things We Do | A Big Innovation Relative to Today | A Major Disruptive Idea |
|---|---|---|---|
| **Possible to Start and Finish this in the Near-Term** |  |  |  |
| **A Longer-Term Horizon to Make It Happen** |  |  |  |
| **Can Start and Finish It Right Away** |  |  |  |

This type of grid becomes the target where your team will share the ideas they select, providing their initial sense of how ideas stack up relative to their potential. You might use multiple prioritization grids, with each one tied to a strategic theme, priority, opportunity, or challenge.

## Individual and Group Perspectives

Speaking of team members, we recommend inviting everyone who participated in generating the original ideas to help prioritize them. With 1,000 ideas, pick 200 as the target number for your team to place on one or more of these Prioritization Grids. You are aiming for 200 because our experience at Brainzooming has shown that, at the high end, 15 to 20 percent of ideas are potentially viable as they emerge from a typical ideation workshop.

To get team members started, divide the 200 ideas by the number of participants. That suggests the maximum number of ideas each member can select for consideration from the 1,000 ideas. We recommend letting people select these ideas individually so there's no convincing or sell-in required to get an idea considered initially. Once they select their ideas, ask them to move them to the prioritization grid, placing each one based on a personal assessment of how innovative it is and the timeframe to accomplish it.

Once the team shares their personal opinions, engage in group discussions. Move ideas on the grid based on where the group agrees you should place them. As you progress through this step, consolidate similar ideas to eliminate duplicates or create mini-concepts from related ideas. If your time is limited at this point, you can always reconvene at another time to complete the work.

### Moving from Deciding to Doing

To accelerate moving from deciding to doing, invite each participant to identify a few ideas or concepts to own in the near-term. This ownership implies nothing more than developing a concept statement for each idea.

The recap needn't be overly-complicated. Perhaps the concept is just one page that highlights the concept's name, a preliminary description, how it delivers benefits, critical success factors for development, and the first five steps to move the concept forward. Inviting those generating the ideas to describe the concepts streamlines the process and creates a true sense of the ideas as they emerged from the team.

As you continue to develop ideas and concepts, you have a robust roadmap for moving your team toward collective recognition for its Idea Magnet-caliber impact.

* * *

An early, decidedly non-Idea Magnet boss used to talk about computer knowledge as a lower-level skill. I thought my boss was full of crap, and embraced learning anything to prepare myself to perform productively. That meant figuring out how to get the most from the clumsy software we had available.

Flash forward a dozen years. I was at work on the Saturday over the July 4 holiday organizing my office. I received an internal phone call from Greg Reid wanting to know my location. I told him I was one floor below him. He said to stay put because he was coming down.

He escorted me to the senior executive offices, closed his door, had me sign a non-disclosure agreement, and informed me the following Tuesday our company was announcing our purchase of a major competitor.

A small group of senior executives was busily working to prepare the announcement, but they hit a snag: no one there that weekend had the PowerPoint and charting skills to create the investor presentations needed for the announcement.

Creating the PowerPoint slides would be my job.

While I was a vice president and heavily involved in market strategy for our multi-billion corporation, I was brought into the inner circle on this billion-dollar acquisition because I knew PowerPoint inside and out. That mastery of lower-level skills was paying off again.

The moral of the story: When you have an opportunity anytime in your career to learn a skill, especially one that allows you to implement things better and more effectively, do it.

You never know how your ability to do even lower-level skills will be what attracts incredible opportunities to contribute to the most important strategic move your organization will ever make!

# 10
# Recharging Creative Energy

There is a baseball truism that, at least for me, relates directly to creativity: "Speed never slumps." This idea suggests that in constructing a solid baseball team, ample speed is vital to success. Pitching, hitting, and other skills can fall apart for players and teams, often with no notice and little explanation. But fast players can—day in and day out—use speed to help the team succeed.

Similarly, innate creativity, along with inspiration and creative energy, can falter. If you depend completely on intangible, amorphous phenomena for creativity, you have to hope they show up and work when you need them. Or you must restrict your creative output to only specific periods when everything is working well.

How about an opposite approach for recharging your creativity? One built around the creative equivalent of speed? It keeps working even as you recharge all the other creative variables in life.

The good news? This approach is what we've been sharing throughout Idea Magnets: A series of strategies built around multiple, varied, and dependable creative thinking formulas, excited and engaged collaborators, and environments that foster new thinking and plentiful ideas daily. Here's one easy way to find material for a creative recharge: Visit IdeaMagnets.com/recharge and download *The Idea Magnets Creative Recharge*. This companion book incorporates the ideas here and adds other fun approaches to recharging creative energy.

## Recharging Your Creative Energy

Idea Magnets create energy for others, which can leave them with a distinct need to replenish their own creative inspirations, inputs, and energy. To do that, you need to recognize when your energy is waning, and allow space for recharging.

Idea Magnets know that what works best for recharging will change over time. They constantly experiment with new methods, identifying what will work better at different times or under new circumstances.

In my corporate career within the transportation industry, we spent considerable time thinking about balance. Whether you're moving things or people, the ideal state is having the same volume arriving (inbound) and departing (outbound) to operate in balance.

If you're too heavy outbound, it means you have lots of things going out, but very few coming in. Heavy inbound is the opposite—many things arriving, but few leaving. Being out of balance for too long creates a litany of challenges and costs, so transportation companies try to actively balance their networks.

Effective management of creative energy requires a similar routine. It's easy to find yourself in creative imbalance, with a disconnect between the amount of creativity you're producing and the creative inspiration that's fueling your energy.

Idea Magnets tend to run heavy on the outbound side. Part of it is simply a personality trait; another is that having tons of ideas is a required part of their jobs. Generating all those ideas is a lot of work—and it presents some obvious challenges.

When a node in a transportation network is too heavy on the outbound side, you begin to face challenges fulfilling your commitments because you lack the necessary resources. Doesn't that sound like an Idea Magnet that is continually transmitting creativity to others while ignoring his or her own creative resource supply?

Similarly, Idea Magnets can be depleted by the *volume* of creative ideas they imagine and share, plus the *number of decisions* they make. An Idea Magnet needs to account for inbound time to absorb, replenish, and learn, unencumbered by the need to directly react to or fuel creativity in others.

One approach is to view creative responsibilities as a repertoire of activities. For me, that includes developing strategies, thinking and reflecting, writing, designing workshops, assembling presentations, creating graphics, traveling, speaking, and many other responsibilities. From among all these duties, I try to shift my attention to the activities that are the easiest to do creatively during any given part of the day.

While sometimes the creative priority is dictated by a deadline, meeting, or other commitment, it's often possible to manage your schedule. You can try picking the creative activity that's easiest to accomplish in the place and time you are right now. If that activity becomes a struggle, change direction to pursue whatever is easiest to accomplish in the moment. In this way, you can manage energy and productivity while maximizing the amount of time spent in creative work.

### Turning to Other Idea Magnets

Idea Magnets can always look to other Idea Magnets for invaluable creative help and new perspectives. I'm always thankful that both familiar and unexpected Idea Magnets seem to continually appear in my professional life to share their enthusiasm and ideas.

Diane Bleck of The Doodle Institute first reached out to me online. She graciously offered to create infographics for several Brainzooming blog articles. On a quick trip to Chicago, Diane agreed to meet with me and another team member. We didn't have any plans for connecting other than to take advantage of proximity to catch up in person. Or at least I didn't!

Diane arrived at our destination and kicked me in the butt in the nicest possible way. She schooled me on her business model and challenged me on why I wasn't doing the same thing. It was just the creativity charge I needed—and hadn't even known I was looking for! With Diane's prompting, I started sketching a visual vocabulary for one of our workshops on the plane ride home. Longer-term, I started to expand our business strategy, developing other platforms for sharing our messages on strategy, creativity, and innovation. This book is one result of the much-needed, Idea-Magnet-kick-in-the-backside Diane delivered.

Are you looking for the Idea Magnets that are present, all around you? They're perfect sources for helping with the creative recharges you need to be the strongest Idea Magnet possible. Personally, my most important Idea Magnet isn't even visible.

Prayer and seeking help from God is integral to my creative energy. I try to dedicate a half-hour to prayer each morning after mass. People who see me in church probably think I have a deep, peaceful prayer life. The truth? Silencing my mind to pray and listen for answers from God is *incredibly* difficult. I spend much of the time struggling to quiet and focus my mind. Nonetheless, prayer and asking God for answers regularly help me in business. The most fruitful prayers involve bringing a conundrum to God, admitting I have no clue about it, and asking for guidance that's consistent with God's will.

You may be doubtful about prayer as a creative tool. Perhaps you're wondering how I could seriously look to prayer as a dependable part of shaping business strategy.

Here are two examples:

Not long after my father passed away, I found myself struggling to develop a sales call script. I noted the irony in this scenario: my dad, the quintessential sales guy, would have been able to help me solve the problem in a heartbeat. Frustrated, I went to bed after midnight, asking God to help me figure out an answer. I added that if my dad could hear me, I needed his help too. Within a few minutes, before falling asleep, the sales script arrived in my mind as though dictated. I wrote it out the next morning and had exactly what I needed.

Another time I needed to communicate a potentially awkward situation to a client. Wrapping up work for the evening, I didn't know what to put in the email. I went to bed and prayed for the words because I could not see a way to explain it. During the night, the exact words came to me.

Those are just two instances. There are many more. Yes, prayer works as a source to replenish your creative energy. And for that, I am very thankful!

I suggest using whatever spirituality resonates with you to recharge your creative potential. Consider this creativity prayer to help focus attention and create personal openness to opportunities for inspiration and quiet reflection.

### *A Creativity Prayer*

*Thank you, Lord, for creation itself and the incredible gifts and talents you so generously entrust to me. May I appreciate and develop these talents, always recognizing that they come from you and remain yours.*

*Guide me in using them for the benefit of everyone that I touch, so that they may be more aware of your creative presence and develop the creativity entrusted to them for the good of others.*

*Help me also to use your talents to bring a creative spark and new possibilities to your world, living out my call to be an integral part of your creative force. Amen.*

\* \* \*

## In Action: Managing and Maximizing Your Creative Energy

Idea Magnets must frequently fashion highly efficient ways to find new creative inspiration quickly. This is often the case at the exact moment when you *feel* least creative. Maybe your job requires daily creativity while offering few opportunities to recharge in dramatic ways. Perhaps your work environment's attitude is less about waiting for creative inspiration and more about, "Be creative NOW, dammit!"

If this sounds familiar, functioning as a high-performing Idea Magnet daily requires continually managing your creative inputs.

### Revisit and Reset Your Creative Backdrop

While the people, places, and situations you turn to for creative energy will be specific to you, the following ideas can expand your range of creative recharge opportunities.

#### Exploit reusable creative structures

A *fake book* is a tool that gives musicians enough of a song's framework (lyrics, melody, chords) to perform at a moment's notice. A creative fake book provides the core of a creative structure that helps individuals quickly go from nothing to creativity. For me, the Brainzooming blog is my creative fake book: when I need a creative structure to get started quickly, I visit the blog at Brainzooming.com/blog. Are you taking advantage of your own personal repertoire of easily-accessed creative tools? It can be a real life saver.

#### Revise your expectations

If your overall creative task seems daunting, revise your expectations. Instead of trying to achieve previous creative pinnacles, look for smaller parts of the project that seem possible and new. Identify workarounds for whatever might be impossible on your project, and go all-out in developing what is achievable creatively.

## Take advantage of the reset that sleep offers

Sleep can help boost your creativity tremendously. Early mornings and late evenings (if they come after a refreshing nap) can provide a fresh view and maximum creative output.

## Redefine your creative game

If the creative task you're facing isn't working, redefine it. Instead of thinking about what the creative activity is, look at what type of goal you're trying to accomplish. Assess the variety of ways you can reach your objective. Redefining the creative game can deliver a valuable win.

## Put a creative project on hold

The pressure for immediate creativity can stifle your abilities. Instead of allowing yourself to be pressured into implementation, take time and *think*. Strategize. Spend time Brainzooming. Let your mind wander where it will, making unconscious creative connections to recharge the creative strategy.

## Get away from the daily routine

Turn your routine upside down, or just make a simple adjustment. Grab your laptop and work from a different location. Switch up your tasks so you start the day with different activities. For me, airplane time is my favorite creative getaway because it is completely disconnected from the daily routine.

## Immerse yourself in inspiring activities

I love riding roller coasters to stimulate creativity. (I just don't get to do it often enough.) Some might enjoy playing sports or attending a live concert. For others, something exciting involves discovering landscapes full of amazing visual stimuli: mountains, oceans, vegetation, extreme conditions, and unique environments. In those natural settings, it's easy for ideas to start flowing because of the inspiration the scenery provides.

* * *

### Borrow Some Kid Creativity

Kids, who are at the creative pinnacles of their lives, naturally explore, try, do the outrageous, and bounce back to create again.

Kid-like behaviors are great for adults to embrace. We can all benefit from recharging our oh-so-serious work lives with the amazing connections and unbridled fun of youth.

- Do something every day that makes you giggle. Better yet, seek out a belly laugh several times a day.
- Take something with you when you're in public to occupy yourself creatively in case you get bored and cranky. (For me, it's something I can use to write or draw.)
- Draw your ideas, even if the lines are crooked or it's tough to tell exactly what it is. And never call it an infographic!
- Crumple up your paper (literally or figuratively) and throw it across the room. Sometimes, it is easier creatively to start from scratch than trying to re-edit or re-format something old to fit in a new situation.

125

- Place toys in plain view in your office. Don't be reluctant to play with them during boring meetings.
- Keep a box of Crayola crayons nearby to color a picture and put it on a wall, backsplash, or file cabinet.
- Make new friends. Seek out those on the fringes of the areas in which you are interested—and even the areas in which you aren't interested.
- Forget to bring your work home with you at day's end. Work on it between meetings. It will probably be better that way, anyway.
- Take a building-block approach when developing a project. Build things in pieces, try out different combinations, take them apart, and reassemble them until something works.

Most important, if you are around kids, ask them how they would approach your creative opportunity. Their answers may inspire you!

* * *

## In Action: Recharging Your Team Members' Creativity

Keeping yourself fully charged creatively is challenging. Managing the recharging needs of a team adds a different level of complexity. You must account for an array of personalities who each have different optimal paths to creative replenishment.

Fortunately, you can apply solo recharging techniques with the *individuals* that make up your team, similar to the way you would add a specific group's spin to the approaches.

## Borrowing Creative Accomplishments

Once, when I was speaking to a graduate class on innovation, a student who was a communications leader at a large tech company talked about his department's "Plagiarism Fridays." They used this as a show-and-tell event to get employees looking at strong creative ideas from other industries, thinking about how their company could learn from them. What a great idea!

You can adapt it to recharge your own team. Block out time to get together. Ask your team to gather examples of creative ideas that appeal to them. The only rule: They must be from outside your industry. For each idea, they should identify what's strong, what's intriguing or unusual, what they would improve, and a recommendation for how your business could incorporate learnings from it. Share the assessments as a group, and apply the ideas to a few of your business challenges. Ideally, you'll be able to move some ideas directly into implementation.

## Sparking a Team's Creative Thinking

In the Midwest, where I grew up, grain elevators are common. These tall structures hold a concentration of grain, which in high volumes can be both combustible and explosive. Given the large, combustible surface area, it only takes a small spark to explode an elevator. Intriguingly, there is a direct parallel between the factors behind explosive conditions in grain elevators *and* your team's creative thinking.

### Large surface area

When it comes to creativity, this translates to setting up many-to-many (as opposed to one-on-one) interactions among team members to energize creative possibilities. In this way, a variety of people are exposed to one another, and can stimulate new thoughts and perspectives across the team.

### Intensity

Achieve intensity by constraining time and creating high expectations for the number of ideas your collection of Idea Magnets might imagine. With just a few competitive people involved across a large group of participants, combining a big goal and a deadline pushes everyone's creative thinking skills for big impact.

### Structure

Finally, creative thinking exercises provide the right structure for team collaboration, sparking explosive ideas from otherwise calm discussions.

When you think about creative techniques to use with your team, look for ways to use these three variables to maximize your team's explosive creativity!

* * *

## Playing Different Creative Parts

In a long-ago Bugs Bunny cartoon titled *Bugs' Bonnets*, Elmer Fudd, Bugs' success-challenged pursuer, dons a variety of different hats as they are blown onto his head. He immediately takes on the persona attached to each hat, changing his wardrobe, attitude, behavior, and interaction with Bugs.

As silly as it sounds, I mention this cartoon frequently when it comes to recharging creative perspectives: give someone an atypical role to expand their creative horizons and watch it energize and recharge your team.

I used this idea with a client seeking bold change from its highly-tenured team. We created four distinct roles for informal facilitators to push the group's innovative thinking in strong, varied ways:

- The Minister of Scare the Crap Out of Us Possibilities (for bursts of extreme creativity)
- Questioner of What We Think (to challenge the status quo)
- The Czar(ina) of Simplification (to find ways to streamline complex ideas)
- The Prince/Princess of Experience (to represent internal customer perspectives)

On the workshop's second day, we added another role: The Queen of Intrigue. That role went to the group's senior executive, to focus the group on transformative ideas.

We asked each person playing a role to identify ways to expand ideas the group was sharing. We provided strategic questions for their own use, including:

- "That's great. How can we do that _____?"
- "What if that were _____?"
- "Ooooh, can we enhance that by _____?"
- "What would it look like if we also _____?"

We also supplied positive, Idea Magnetizing prompts to fill in the blanks in the questions.

When you try this, dole out the roles so that they genuinely stretch each individual and force them to look at the project, your organization, and your customers in dramatically new ways. If someone feels uncomfortable with an assigned role, remind them that everybody's likely uncomfortable, and that you will rotate the roles (or maybe create new ones) next time.

This approach is really another way to generate excitement about imagining ideas—and will help your team recharge at the same time.

\* \* \*

As an Idea Magnet, remember: you can't recognize when one of your team members needs to recharge if you aren't replenishing your own creativity. That means doing more than superficially taking care of yourself. You need to set the example for your team. They need to clearly see that you value self-care. Invite them to join you in regularly replenishing their creative energies. Encourage speaking up when they need to take breaks.

And, importantly, make sure you listen and take action when everyone around you is saying that you need to recharge. When the universe appears to be repeatedly reminding you that it is time to chill, step back and implement the simple steps that you know will work best for you and take the time to recharge yourself.

# 11

# Closing the Circuit

As you continue your journey of growth as an Idea Magnet surrounded by other Idea Magnets, remember this: significant creative learning and accomplishments await you in life's most humble moments. That's why they are so easy for most people to overlook.

## Inspiration and Golden Opportunities

We have all heard Aesop's fable about the goose who laid eggs that were encased in gold. As a child, my takeaway from the story, and maybe yours too, was that the golden eggs in life—the incredible opportunities— would be blatantly obvious. You would easily see that while eggs are generally white, blue, or brown, a select few were gold. The golden ones would be valuable; the others would be nothing special.

Then, a few years ago, I was facilitating an innovation workshop at a Marriott in Oak Brook, Illinois. Down the hall from our workshop, an art installation called *Travel* stopped me dead in my tracks. The piece, by

Allan Howze, contained dozens of white-shelled eggs, broken open, and affixed to a black background.

And the inside of each eggshell was coated in gloriously shiny gold.

Looking at that piece over the course of a few days influenced me profoundly. For the first time, I imagined more distinctly that the incredible opportunities in life could appear with the plainest trappings. The experience provided a wake-up call for me, very much in the Idea Magnet style, to start noticing the potential impact in the moments I'd previously considered mundane.

### Attracting Others Who Pass By

Just as plain eggshells can hide golden eggs, extraordinary people can also appear in otherwise ordinary circumstances.

One day as I visited with my mother-in-law, Pat, at a senior living facility in Western Kansas, I heard another resident telling a staff member about the WPA (Works Progress Administration) and the Depression. The opportunity to hear firsthand from someone who lived events most of us read about in books or see on documentaries drew me in. Between that opportunity and learning more about Harry's creative talent, I wound up spending most of the afternoon with him.

Harry was a World War II veteran. He made it all the way to Berlin. While he talked some about his experiences both before and during the early parts of the war, he didn't want to speak about his experiences at the end of World War II.

He was more open in talking about his lifelong love of exercise and art. He told us of still getting out whenever the weather is nice to walk around the senior center's perimeter. Most enthusiastically, he talked about how much he loved to draw and sketch. Harry shared about the gift he'd been given to be able to see something and draw it. I asked to see his drawings, but he said he usually threw them away when they were done. He admitted that his daughter got after him for it, but contended that he could always make more drawings.

I asked him if we could draw some things together. We lacked nice drawing paper, but there were plenty of paper towels available. Presented with individual sheets of paper towel, Harry was off and drawing. As the afternoon progressed, he recreated drawings he'd done before and thrown away. He sketched memories of things he had built, and he shared his wisdom from 90+ years.

I'm so happy that Harry's WPA story attracted my attention that Saturday afternoon. He created the space and the occasion to share ideas, talents, and encouragement for life, just as an Idea Magnet does.

## A Simple Creative Leadership Formula

At the church I attend on Sundays, they begin praying the rosary thirty minutes before mass begins. For the 7 a.m. mass, the rosary crowd is usually small, especially when the weather is bad. One snowy day, we arrived and took a spot near the prayer leader. When a group recites the rosary, the leader typically says the first half of each prayer. The others present recite the second half. This works with even a small group. With only a few people scattered around a large church, it makes the call and response challenging. This is especially true for the leader, who can't hear when people positioned far away complete their half of a prayer.

The fact that we were near the leader helped create some volume for the responses to help him keep pace. When we completed the rosary, the leader stopped to thank us for being there, saying, "It's always easier to lead the rosary when you are here to pray along." I thanked him for showing up early to lead us.

It struck me that this simple situation underscored the way leaders and followers can create and support success for one other. The leader performed his role by:

- Being visible and present, so we knew where to find him
- Getting things started, even though the situation was less than ideal
- Pressing on, no matter what
- Thanking everyone for participating

We, the followers, were also active participants, supporting the leader by:

- Positioning ourselves near the leader
- Dependably carrying out our designated roles
- Being vocal and available to help the leader more effectively perform his part
- Thanking our leader for leading

While there may be all kinds of other moving parts within a team, if you, whether as a leader or a follower, can get your four items right, you're well down the path toward success.

### Yes, You ARE an Idea Magnet

I share these stories in closing because of the common reminder in these otherwise mundane moments: Idea Magnets are all around us, in individuals, organizations (small and large), works of art, and anything else that inspires our creativity and innovative spirit.

Importantly, Idea Magnets need others, and we all need more Idea Magnets. That's your calling. You're an Idea Magnet.

Take the ideas shared here, and all the ones you imagine and learn in the world, and be the force for amazing creativity you have always been destined to be!

# 12
## What's Next?

Congratulations, and thanks for reading all the way to the end of *Idea Magnets*! Wait a minute. You did read to the end, right? Or did you come here first? Or maybe you skipped around and just happened to wind up at the end?

If that's the case, then you really ARE an Idea Magnet, finding the best path to keep your creativity charged. Good for you!

If you found your way here looking for more information on Idea Magnets and what we do at The Brainzooming Group to help organizations to enhance their strategies and boost innovation, you are in the right place.

### Want to Find Out More about Me?

Seriously? After reading the whole book, you want to learn more about me? Wow, thanks!

I founded The Brainzooming™ Group in 2009 to lead organizations in creating strategic impact and outstanding results with innovative ideas. We're honored to work with companies and nonprofits across a variety of industries in the US and beyond. Additionally, I speak frequently on multiple topics to help individuals become immediately more successful by better applying their knowledge and innate creativity. Brainzooming.com, our blog, reaches readers in nearly two hundred countries annually who are looking for actionable ideas on strategy, innovation, and branding.

### Want to Learn More about *Idea Magnets*?

If you want to grab additional actionable tools and resources to grow your creative talents and those of your team, visit IdeaMagnets.com. There you can access *The Idea Magnets Creative Recharge* guide to help you on your journey, learn more ideas on applying strategic thinking and creativity in your workplace, find links to all our online presences, and stay up-to-date on *Idea Magnets* activities. You can order additional copies of the book, including in bulk if you want to get copies for your team!

### Want to Bring *Idea Magnets* to your Organization?

One of the best ways to energize your team's creativity is with a live *Idea Magnets* keynote or training workshop. Available in one-hour to multi-day formats, we can take your team, organization, or conference attendees through the Idea Magnet strategies and tools to become stronger creative leaders and innovators. Among the most popular topics are:

- *Idea Magnets – 7 Strategies for Cultivating & Attracting Creative Business Leaders*
- *Disruptive Thinking – Unexpected Connections & Polar Opposites that Energize Creativity*

- *Positively Charged – Conducting Big Breakthroughs from Small Ideas*
- *Idea Magnetism – Charging Your Organization for Success*
- *Generate! Making Tried & True, Improved & New Ideas Flow*

Learn more at IdeaMagnets.com/speaking and let's develop the right program for you!

### Looking to Get Your Organization Brainzooming?

If the time is right to strengthen your organization's strategy, The Brainzooming™ Group can design and lead your entire team through a dynamic process using our strategic thinking tools to increase collaboration, save time in planning, and deliver actionable, results-oriented strategies. To talk through your needs and how we can help, contact us at info@brainzooming.com.

### Have ideas on collaborating?

Email me at collaborate@ideamagnets.com, and let's imagine what amazing things we can do together. I'm looking forward to connecting with you!

# Acknowledgements

Thank you to God, my wife Cyndi (who was the Idea
Magnet who brought me back to God), and
my mom and dad.

All the Idea Magnets that have blessed me with their
influence and sharing their perspectives have
my ongoing gratitude, because I revisit their
lessons all the time.

Reviewing my career, at least one hundred people have
played a role in defining me, as you learned in Chapter 8.
Another group of people influenced Brainzooming
content since before I launched the company. It would
take hundreds of pages to detail how each of them are
with me daily in spirit.

*Idea Magnets* marks a distinct departure in my thinking
and writing on creativity, innovation, and leadership.
A small group was critical in moving this work ahead:

Lynn Brown-Reyes requested I deliver a
creative leadership webinar that led to the first
Idea Magnets presentation.

Leslie Adams' photography inspired a markedly new look and approach to the Idea Magnets message and tone.

Brian Everett and Dino Moler supported the Idea Magnets topic and recognized its potential during its formative stages.

Emma Alvarez Gibson is the Idea Magnet who provides unwavering encouragement, inspiring better ways of communicating the concepts, sharing her talents in patiently editing revisions on top of revisions. Most importantly, she challenges me if I ever waiver in fully living out the strategies in this book.

Kelly Landry was in the right seat on the wrong flight and struck up a conversation that spawned a friendship that led me to Tara Baukus Mello, who is my consulting editor. Through expertise, prayerfulness, and perseverance, Tara embraced creatively changing how she typically works to cheerlead and nurture me through completing this book.

My huge thanks to all of you!

Made in the USA
Columbia, SC
30 October 2021

48001995R00080